THE DRISKILL HOTEL

Stories of Austin's Legendary Hotel | *A Cookbook for Special Occasions*

THE DRISKILL HOTEL

Stories of Austin's Legendary Hotel | *A Cookbook for Special Occasions*

by Chef David J. Bull

and Turk Pipkin

Book Design and Production, Action Figure

Photography, Mark Knight

Assistant Photography, Taggart Sorensen

Edited by Martha C. Collins

opposite page - In true Texan style, the modern-day Driskill Grill dining room is overlooked by historic Texas governors, Ma & Pa Ferguson.

this page - The historic Driskill Lobby, c. 1930.

THE DRISKILL HOTEL: *Stories of Austin's Legendary Hotel / A Cookbook for Special Occasions*

Copyright ©2005 by The Driskill

ISBN: 0-9765312-0-8

Library of Congress Control Number: 2005921865

Published in the United States by:

THE DRISKILL HOTEL
604 Brazos Street
Austin, TX 78701
www.driskillhotel.com

Designed and produced by:

ACTION FIGURE
109 East Tenth Street
Austin, Texas 78701
www.actionfigure.com

First Edition

dedication

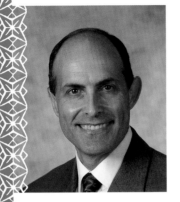

THE FACT that The Driskill Hotel exists today is a testament to many fine men and women. We dedicate this book to those past and present visionaries who physically created and emotionally bestowed The Driskill with her timeless soul.

We honor all those who invested their time and resources in the hotel, and have shared the results with so many guests and visitors since its opening in 1886.

Special thanks to:

☞ R. Max Brooks and the Executive Committee of The Driskill Hotel Corporation who initiated the refinancing plan that ultimately saved The Driskill from certain demolition in 1970.

☞ The citizens of Austin who have supported the hotel through the years and bought stock in The Driskill Hotel Corporation as a philanthropic investment.

☞ The Austin Heritage Society and Heritage Guild whose members created the 1886 Lunch Room and who played an instrumental part in purchasing and promoting the sale of stock.

☞ Brothers Property Corporation, the real estate development company that coordinated the purchase of The Driskill in 1995 with the bold plan to completely restore the legendary hotel.

☞ Lowe Enterprises Investors and Destination Hotels & Resorts, the owners and caretakers of The Driskill who are committed to continue her restoration and traditions of fine hospitality.

☞ The caring professionals who have worked at The Driskill Hotel throughout the years and without whom the magic of the building would have never been realized.

Respectfully,

Jeffrey M. Trigger
Managing Director

DRISKILL HOTEL

BUILT 1885-86 BY COL. JESSE L.
DRISKILL (1824-1890), CATTLE KING
WHO MOVED TO AUSTIN IN 1869.
BRICK DRESSED WITH LIMESTONE.
HAD THREE GRAND ENTRANCES--ONE
THE LARGEST ARCHED DOORWAY IN
TEXAS. "LADIES' ENTRANCE" WAS ON
NORTHEAST. BUST OF COL. DRISKILL
IS OVER SOUTH ARCH, BUSTS OF HIS
RANCHER SONS ON EAST AND WEST.
RICH FURNISHINGS WERE SELECTED
BY COL. DRISKILL, WHO LEASED OUT
HIS HOTEL--SOUTHWEST'S FINEST
WHEN IT OPENED, CHRISTMAS 1886.

RECORDED TEXAS HISTORIC LANDMARK-1966

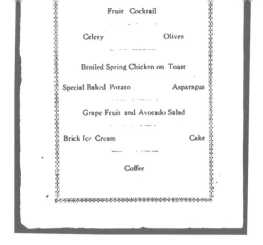

table of contents

introduction

A GRAND DINING TRADITION

From the day The Driskill opened in 1886, great food has been one of the hotel's principle offerings. Spending a grand total of 35 cents on a full meal in the early years, hotel patrons naturally expected something out of the ordinary. The original Driskill kitchen was situated in a separate three-story building adjacent to the hotel's north side, allowing Austin's prevailing southerly breezes to carry the smells of food (and those of the adjacent laundry) away from the guest rooms. In keeping with Colonel Driskill's commitment to the best of everything, the equipment in that kitchen was furnished by the John Van Range Company of Cincinnati, Ohio.

Menus of the late nineteenth century were generally based on the availability of fresh local ingredients, but by taking advantage of Austin's rail service The Driskill was able to offer dishes never before served in the city.

In 1890, the hotel's dinner menu included Greer turtle, trout, filet of Kansas City beef, new potatoes, charlotte of pineapple, asparagus and Edam cheese.

By 1894, raw oysters had appeared on the menu along with roast ribs of beef, corn bread, mashed potatoes and port wine. Already known for delectable desserts, The Driskill was then serving cream pie, mince pie, lemon ice cream and English plum pudding.

For the next sixty years, The Driskill's restaurant would remain an Austin favorite for visitors and locals alike. But despite the popularity of its food, The Driskill did not boast a chef of national acclaim until 1952 when well-known dietician and chef Helen Corbitt was hired to oversee all food and beverage service at the hotel. More than fifty years later, Corbitt's reputation for tradition and innovation is little diminished. Considered the Julia Child of American cuisine, Corbitt combined the freshest ingredients with a great sense of style and imaginative use of unusual flavor combinations.

At The Driskill, Corbitt lived on the second floor in what is now the Heritage Suite, and her food did much to generate a surge of popularity and acclaim for the hotel. Though Corbitt relocated to Dallas in 1955 where she created the Zodiac Room at Neiman Marcus, many of her recipes — including her famous cheese soup served at the 1886 Café & Bakery — are now considered timeless Driskill classics.

THE TRADITION GROWS

EXTENSIVE RENOVATIONS AND RESTORATION of the hotel in recent years have resulted in significant improvements to the overall food experience at The Driskill. Combining a respect for the building's historic past with a vision for an ever-improving food experience has resulted in a series of positive changes for the grande dame of Austin dining.

The redesign and reopening of The 1886 Café & Bakery is a good example of this principle at work. The new bakery kitchen — visible through glass windows from the seating area, which also overlooks bustling Sixth Street — turns out some of Austin's finest wedding and birthday cakes, delectable sweets, pastries and breads. At the same time, the cafe has its own full-service kitchen serving three meals a day, seven days a week, starting at dawn and serving until midnight on weekends.

"The cafe gives us a great opportunity to create a casual menu with the finest of ingredients and offers Austin a quick and valuable dining experience," says The Driskill's Executive Chef David J. Bull.

Since the hotel has a wide range of culinary demands, The 1886 Café kitchen also caters room service, while another new kitchen on the second floor provides for banquets and catering.

These unseen changes have left The Driskill Grill with an extensive kitchen dedicated exclusively to serving dinner five nights a week. Six chefs working in harmony in this spacious kitchen turn out some of the most incredible food in central Texas. Each evening, Chef Bull and his Executive Sous Chef, Josh Watkins, work together to make sure every ingredient is checked, every component is tasted and every staff member is ready for another exciting evening of service.

"It's important to set a consistent standard and to explain that standard and how to achieve it to the entire staff," says Chef Bull.

Because Bull believes the culinary team is the most important ingredient in any kitchen, he's gone to great lengths to put together one of the best teams in the country.

"The keys to success are training, teaching, motivation, understanding, and passion," Bull stresses. "After that, the food comes naturally because each person strives for perfection every night."

The Driskill Grill offers a variety of dishes that are meant to stimulate the palate and create a dining experience that exceeds all expectations. The Grill's staff takes pride in using the best of ingredients, continually perfecting their culinary techniques, and using simple flavors, natural combinations and artful presentations designed to feed your mind, body and emotions. Attention to detail — attractive presentation, impeccably prepared cuisine and unpretentious but informative service — has helped The Driskill elevate hospitality to an art form. And for its great contribution in setting this higher dining standard, The Driskill has received an enormous amount of national recognition.

The Driskill Grill dining room, pictured here c. 1963, continues to provide an elegant dining ambiance for hotel guests, native Austinites, and world travelers alike.

top right - Victorian Suite, today.

The sight of The Driskill at what was then the corner of East Pecan (foreground) and Brazos and what is now Sixth Street and Brazos.

Colonel Driskill (1824–1890)

This life-size portrait of Colonel Driskill was painted four months after his death by celebrated Austin artist W.H. Huddle whose paintings throughout the Texas Capitol include famous representations of Davy Crockett and the surrender of Santa Anna in 1836. Presented to The Driskill Hotel in memory of its founder, the painting of Colonel Driskill occupies a place of honor on The Driskill landing overlooking the hotel lobby.

history

THE VISION OF JESSE LINCOLN DRISKILL

"No shrewder cattleman ever put brand to a yearling."
— The Fort Worth Democrat

Austin has long been a place of vision and creativity. To locate the capital city of a new nation on a dangerous frontier required extraordinary vision. For the past century and a half, creativity has been the guiding force that helped the city grow into a world-renowned center for education, the arts and high-tech innovation.

Long before Austin achieved an international reputation for its vibrant filmmaking community, before its designation as "the live music capital of the world," and before a University of Texas student named Michael Dell began making and selling personal computers out of his dorm room, one man's vision resulted in a great architectural treasure that would play a key role in the future of Austin.

Like most Texans of his day, Colonel Jesse Lincoln Driskill was not a native of the new Lone Star state. Born in Tennessee in 1924 -and reportedly named for his family's friend, Abraham Lincoln - Driskill came to Texas in 1849. After a brief career as a merchant and his marriage to the daughter of a Texas rancher, Driskill became one of the first cattlemen to move herds of longhorns north through Indian country. During the Civil War, he made a fortune selling cattle to the Confederacy, then promptly went bust when his Confederate currency became worthless. Left with only his honorary military title, Colonel Driskill promptly made another fortune driving large herds of cattle to railheads in Kansas.

In 1869, Driskill moved with his wife and four daughters from Bastrop to Austin, which he believed - despite the rough-and-tumble town having only 4,000 residents at the time - would soon be one of America's great cities. His timing could not have been better, for the first railroad reached Austin in 1871, and one year later a statewide election made permanent Austin's previously temporary status as the Capital of Texas. By the end of the decade, Austin had grown to a burgeoning city of 11,000, larger than both Dallas and Fort Worth.

As if to prove his faith in his new hometown, in 1881 Driskill built Austin's most magnificent home, a palatial structure with 20-inch thick brick walls, a billiard room on the third floor and indoor plumbing - the first in town.

Though the Colonel's home at 2610 Whitis was razed in 1963, the old cattleman's next visionary Austin structure would see a finer fate.

A GRAND HOTEL IN THE HEART OF TEXAS

Humble Beginnings

1824 - *Jesse Lincoln Driskill is born in Sparta, Tennessee.*

1836 - *Texas becomes an independent Nation, the Republic of Texas.*

1838 - *Mirabeau B. Lamar, Vice President of Texas, sees buffalo roaming the banks of the Colorado in a spot he will soon suggest as the future Capital of Texas.*

1839 - *The Texas Congress convenes in Austin for the first time.*

1840 - *Edwin Waller is elected first mayor of Austin with 187 votes.*

1845 - *Texas joins the union and Austin is named the state capital through 1850.*

1849 - *Jesse Driskill moves to Texas and settles in Bastrop.*

1850 - *Austin's population is 629.*

1850 - *A statewide election chooses Austin as the state capital for another twenty years.*

1857 - *Jesse Driskill enters the cattle business, moving herds of cattle north through Indian country.*

1860 - *Austin's population is 3,500.*

1860-1865 - *Jesse Driskill makes a fortune in cattle, but loses it when his Confederate currency becomes worthless.*

1869 - *Jesse Driskill moves to Austin, the westernmost metropolis in Texas.*

1870 - *Austin's population is 4,400.*

1871 - *The first railway - Houston and Texas Central Railroad - reaches Austin.*

1872 - *A statewide election permanently establishes Austin as the capital of Texas.*

Having spent much of his life traveling from town to town on the wagon roads and cattle trails of Texas, J.L. Driskill knew the capital city of Texas needed a grand hotel which could serve as the center of business, politics and society. The great dream of Driskill's life was to build that hotel. The first public notice regarding the dream becoming a reality appeared in the Austin Daily American on June 19, 1884.

"Col. J.L. Driskill has signified his willingness to pay $7,500 for the lot and building at Bois d'Arc (7th Street). Austin can now congratulate herself at the prospects of a first class hotel."

The hotel's designer would be Jasper Preston of the local architecture firm, J.N. Preston and Sons. The designer of the impressive Walter Tips Building at 712 Congress, Preston had also served on the jury that chose Elijah Myer's Renaissance Revival design for the State Capitol building, which was already under construction.

Having moved to Austin from New York a decade earlier, Preston had seen a number of buildings designed by famed architect Henry Hobson Richardson whose work had modernized the round arches and heavy columns of the Romanesque architectural style with detailed rock-face masonry, open arches, and a great sense of weight and solidity. Inspired by these ideas, Preston turned out a spectacular design for The Driskill. Though just four stories high, the building seems to soar out of the ground, with the vast rounded arches of its three main entrances repeated above in a gradually diminishing scale. Attention to exterior details included columns, corbels, caps and gargoyles.

"Warm, romantic, and protecting," Preston's design was called, a description that would seem ideal for any timeless hotel.

Covering half a city block, the building was to measure 150 feet on East Pecan (now known as Sixth Street), 260 feet on the west side, 80 feet on East Bois d'Arc

(now Seventh Street), and a 170-foot strip on Brazos Street. The official cornerstone was laid in January, 1885. In August, the temporary framing supporting the giant arch of the main entrance was removed, generating a fair amount of wagering among local gamblers on whether the largest arched doorway in Texas would stand alone as designed.

Driskill had contracted with local brick manufacturer H.A. Thason to fire six million pressed bricks for the structure, while the heavy cast iron columns that would soon support the large interior galleries were shipped to Austin by rail.

Work proceeded fairly smoothly for the next year, but on January 29, 1886, workers were installing the stone columns of the fourth floor verandahs when a construction derrick fell with a thundering crash into East Pecan Street, tearing down telegraph wires and a barbershop awning and landing on a delivery wagon parked in front of the Phi Abram Grocery store. One of the two horses hitched to the wagon was killed instantly, but no people were injured.

By March, work was under way on the interior plastering and woodwork, which was made of the highest-quality long-leaf yellow pine from East Texas and Louisiana, all of it secured by square-headed nails. Determined to use only the highest-quality materials, Colonel Driskill had already departed for the East Coast to purchase glass, hardware and tile with which to complete his dream.

J. W. "Bud" DRISKILL
Brazos Street Entrance

Bud Driskill

Final personal touches above the exterior arches included carved stone busts of Jesse Driskill and his sons, Tobe and Bud, along with the carved heads of Texas longhorns, untold thousands of which had been the source of the $400,000 that Driskill spent on the building of his dream.

UNVEILING A WORK OF ART

"Hospitality is the truest impulse of the human heart."

— Austin Daily Statesman, Driskill Grand Opening Edition, December 17, 1886

Austin's future had never shone so brightly as on December 20, 1886, opening day of the eagerly awaited Driskill Hotel. Lining the street by the thousands as they awaited their turn to pass through the grand entrance on Pecan Street, Austinites whetted their appetites for the wonders inside by reading the eight-page supplement to the Austin Daily Statesman, 20,000 copies of which had been circulated to celebrate the big day.

Packed with laudatory adjectives, the newspaper described everything from the "principal facade of pressed brick dressed with white limestone" to the "system of bells connecting by means of an electric button to every room." Even the billiard parlor received special notice, particularly the walls overlooking the tables which sported "the head of an immense Texas steer with its huge horns spanning five feet."

Having completed its descriptions of the hotel's luxurious appointments, the Austin Daily Statesman proudly announced that:

"The Driskill will be opened to receive guests Monday, December 20th, which day will commence a new era in the history of Austin."

West of Saint Louis and east of San Francisco, The Driskill knew no peer. Within weeks, the hotel would assume its role as the center of Austin's social and political scene when it hosted the inaugural ball of newly elected Governor Sul Ross, beginning a tradition of gubernatorial celebrations that would last for decades. So fully did The Driskill fill the gap as the hotel of Austin that no other major hotel would be built in the growing city for another forty years.

Steam heat, gas chandeliers and a hydraulic elevator - to the citizens of Austin, these were all new wonders, the harbinger of a new day for a town still considered a frontier capital complete with a reputation for drinking, gambling and prostitution.

The first floor of the hotel had corridors more than 30 feet wide with black slate and marble floors passing between billiard and bar rooms, a barber shop and an office and reception desk located at the intersection of the main corridors. In addition to 20-foot ceilings on the first floor, the hotel centerpiece was a four-story rotunda topped by a stained-glass skylight that brought light and cooling breezes to the entire hotel.

The second floor featured a grand dining room, a more informal club dining room, two large parlors, and several hotel rooms, including two bridal apartments. The third and fourth floors were devoted entirely to guest rooms, all with heavy walnut wardrobes large enough to hold a hoop skirt or even a saddle.

The entire structure was designed to be virtually fireproof, with continuous brick partition walls running from foundation to roof, and with every ceiling of corrugated iron sandwiched between three-inch layers of cement.

The first floor of the hotel had corridors more than 30 feet wide with black slate and marble floors passing between billiard and bar rooms, a barber shop and an office and reception desk located at the intersection of the main corridors.

1880 - *Austin's population reaches 11,000.*

1881 - *The University of Texas is established by an act of the legislature.*

1882 - *Construction begins on the new capitol building.*

1884 - *J.L. Driskill purchases a lot at the corner of Brazos and Pecan (later renamed Sixth Street).*

1885 - *Construction begins on The Driskill.*

1886 - *Grand opening of The Driskill, called by the Austin Daily Statesman, "One of the Finest Hotels in the Whole Country."*

January 1887 - *Less than two weeks after its grand opening, The Driskill hosts its first inaugural ball for newly elected Texas Governor Sul Ross.*

May 1887 - *The Driskill is closed briefly when key hotel staff members are hired away by Galveston's Beach Hotel.*

Spring 1888 - *J.L. Driskill's loses 3,000 cattle to a late-season blizzard.*

THE DRISKILL.

WHAT A BONANZA AUSTIN

POSSESSES IN ITS NEW

CARAVANSARY.

April 1888 - *The Hotel is closed when Colonel Driskill is nearly bankrupted by cattle losses due to freeze and drought. Unable to cover his debt, Driskill sells his new hotel to his son-in-law J.M. "Doc" Day for $350,000.*

May 1888 - *The hotel is reopened by Doc Day in time to host international dignitaries for the dedication of the new state capitol.*

A decade after it opened, The Driskill had become the prime gathering place for Austinites who came often for meals, drinks, a shave or a haircut, to bank (near right) or send a telegram, or merely to have their laundry done.

above - Looking north up Brazos.
far right - 1886 Lunch Room
(now The 1886 Café & Bakery).

UPS AND DOWNS AT THE PRIDE OF AUSTIN

In addition to great fanfare, The Driskill opened to solid business from patrons arriving in Austin by rail, on horseback or in carriages which used the hotel's dedicated livery entrance on the west side, or on the stagecoach from San Antonio which ran directly to the hotel. Not only was The Driskill considered the finest hotel in the state, the food was reputed to be the best to be found this side of New Orleans, while The Driskill Drug Store Fountain served "the finest glass of soda in the city."

Colonel Driskill managed to overcome his first disaster when the hotel's popular Manager S.E. McIheney and half of his staff departed for greener pastures at Galveston's Beach Hotel (which would be destroyed by fire in 1898). Having lost almost all his key employees, Colonel Driskill simply shuttered his hotel until reopening with new management.

Colonel Driskill's next trial, unfortunately, would prove more disastrous. Because of his extensive ranch and cattle operations, the old Colonel had fully expected to be able to weather any adverse financial conditions at his beloved hotel, even with rooms renting for just $2 to $5 per night and full course meals going for thirty-five cents.

But in the spring of 1888, a severe, late-season blizzard caught Driskill's herd of 3,000 cattle, which were being driven north to his ranch in the Dakotas. So severe was this freeze that almost the entire herd was killed. After the loss of the cattle, coupled with losses due to an extended drought and loans he'd made to other cattlemen, Driskill found himself on the verge of bankruptcy. Just two years after opening his beloved hotel, the Colonel was forced to sell.

The hotel's new owner, Driskill's son-in-law J.M. "Doc" Day, reopened the hotel in time to host a large number of international dignitaries for the dedication of the new Texas capitol.

Despite the success of these festivities, Doc Day quickly learned what several other owners would soon discover - that it wasn't a simple thing to make money with a heavy debt load and a grand hotel to sustain in a town of 15,000 people. In 1893, Day traded the hotel for a California ranch and vineyard plus $14,000 in cash. The new owner, M.B. Curtis, was an actor with the unlikely name of Sam'l of Posen. Lasting less than a year, Posen sold the hotel to a group of New York investors.

The next owner, Major George W. Littlefield, would fare better. Crippled in the Civil War, Littlefield - like Jesse Lincoln Driskill - had made his fortune in the cattle business. Sharing Driskill's vision for the city of Austin, Littlefield had founded American National Bank in the southeast corner of The Driskill's main floor.

Under Littlefield's stewardship, the hotel finally came into its own. An electrical system was installed, with lighting fixtures that used a combination of electricity and gas. Many of those same fixtures, later converted to electricity only, are still seen throughout the hotel. Lavatories and bathtubs were installed in 28 rooms and suites and handsome frescoes were added in every room and corridor.

A decade after it opened, The Driskill had become the prime gathering place for Austinites who came often for meals, drinks, a shave or a haircut, to bank or send a telegram, or merely to have their laundry done.

And just three months before the beginning of the twentieth century, on October 10, 1899 the Southwestern Telephone Company inaugurated its interstate telephone line at The Driskill. Thousands attended a "Grand Blow-out" party to celebrate. For the first time in history, Austin was connected to the world by voice. What wonders could possibly be next?

Spring 1888 - *The Driskill is closed when Colonel Driskill is nearly bankrupted by cattle losses due to freeze and drought.*

May 1888 - *Sold to J.N. "Doc" Day, The Driskill reopens in time to host international dignitaries for the dedication of the new State Capitol, deemed the "the 7th largest building in the world."*

May 1890 - *Colonel Driskill dies of a stroke.*

1891 - *Electric streetcars make their Austin debut, running from Congress Avenue to the new subdivision, Hyde Park.*

1890 - *Austin's population is 15,000.*

1893 - *Doc Day trades the hotel for a California ranch and vineyard.*

1893 - *Austin's "Great Granite Dam," is completed, a milestone in the city's growth.*

1894 - *The Driskill is sold at auction for $76,000 to a group of New York investors, then sold again to the British mortgage holders.*

1894 - *William Sydney Porter - later known as O'Henry - begins publication of his weekly newspaper, The Rolling Stone. It is Porter who first describes Austin as "The City of the Violet Crown."*

1895 - *Major George W. Littlefield pays $116,000 cash for The Driskill.*

1898 - *William Sydney Porter is convicted of swindling funds from the First National Bank and begins serving a three-year prison term.*

1898 - *District attorney Albert S. Burleson announces to Governor C.A. Culberson in The Driskill hotel that he is prepared to raise and mount a company of armed cavalry for the Spanish American War in Cuba.*

1899 - *(Above) Abe Frank's cigar stand opens in the hotel lobby. Over the next 25 years, Frank (with customer) will sell an estimated 4 million cigars — 438 a day.*

ARTESIAN WELLS & HEALING WATERS

With the abundance of clear flowing springs having been one of the main reasons for the city's location, it was no surprise that both hot and cold springs were discovered during the construction of The Driskill. Capitalizing on the healthful qualities of these waters, a variety of healers, medicine men and quacks were attracted to The Driskill, which they used as a base of operations for their unregulated cure-alls.

In 1893, Dr. R.C. Flower arrived in Austin by private railroad car and established a medical practice at The Driskill that he would three years later claim to be the largest in the world. That practice was soon taken over by his brother, Dr. H.A. Flower, who claimed he could diagnose ailments by "psychometric power."

Perhaps seeing that the suckers were ripe for the fleecing, "the World's Invincible Magnetic Healer" Dr. Franklin Stuart Temple moved into The Driskill and began public healings of the deaf, the mute and the blind at Millett's Opera House on Ninth Avenue. In his suite at The Driskill, Temple's private patients were diagnosed by the "World's Renowned Sight-Diagnostician," Professor W. Fletcher Hall. Patients then were ushered in to Dr. Temple where "vital magnetism was transferred to the affected part of the patient," and where the vital contents of the patient's wallet were transferred to Dr. Temple.

By 1900, either the hotel had outgrown its water supply or the springs were drying up. Following the temporary fix of a six-inch water main connecting The Driskill to a larger spring in the basement of the Brueggerhoff Building at Tenth and Congress, drilling was begun on a new artesian well. It was drilled more than 2,000 feet deep and delivered what the hotel referred to as "healing hot waters."

In 1906, Chris Kofahl, the proprietor of The Driskill Barber Shop and Ladies Hairdressing Parlor, installed electric baths and electric body massage. Even the Turkish bath at the barbershop on neighboring Congress Avenue used The Driskill's "hot sulphur water," claiming that it was "long known to contain medical properties second to none in Texas."

RESIDENT FOR LIFE

Peter J. Lawless, general passenger and ticket agent for International and Great Northern Railroad, moved into The Driskill on opening day in 1886 and continued to reside in the hotel until his death an astounding fifty years later. Even when the hotel was closed for extended periods during its early years, Lawless kept his own key and continued to live in the empty building. During his first thirty years in the hotel, Lawless was said to have spent $25,000 on board, enough to have built a small hotel of his own. It's possible the total room bill for his life was double that amount as Lawless would remain a guest at the hotel until his death, some time after the opening of The Driskill annex in 1930.

There are those who believe Lawless - or his ghost to be more precise - continues to reside at the hotel to this day. The ghosts of Lawless and Colonel Driskill, who some claim to detect by the passing faint odor of his ever-present cigar are also said to keep company with the ghost of Mrs. Bridge, a former housekeeper who was never quite happy with the floral arrangements and seems to make constant changes to them.

"PPP - Prickly Ash, Poke Root and Potassium. Best Blood Purifier in the World."

- The supposed contents of a popular
patent medicine later shown to
contain mostly alcohol.

1900 - *Austin Dam is destroyed by a flood on the Colorado River. Austin's population is 22,000.*

1901 - *A crowd of thousands watches President William McKinley parade up Congress Avenue to the Capitol four months before McKinley is assassinated.*

1903 - *Major Littlefield sells The Driskill to Edward Seeling.*

1905 - *Pecan Street in front of the hotel is paved, in bricks, for the first time.*

1908 - *Daughters of the Republic under the leadership of Clara Driscoll meets at The Driskill in a politically divisive battle over preservation of the Alamo in San Antonio.*

November 1908 - *Election returns for William Howard Taft's defeat of William Jennings Bryan for the presidency are projected by Steropticon across Sixth Street from The Driskill.*

1910 - *Austin has its first automobile fatality. Population is 30,000.*

1913 - *Satex Film Company produces "Their Lives By a Thread," the first motion picture made in Austin.*

1913 - *Mayor A. P. Woolridge closes Guy Town, an infamous red light district south of Fifth Street and west of Colorado.*

1916 - *Electricity is added throughout The Driskill Hotel.*

1918 - *Austinites vote for a prohibition on all alcohol sales.*

1918 - *The City of Austin acquires Barton Springs.*

1930 - *A second tower of modern rooms is built alongside the original hotel.*

1931 - *Young Louis Armstrong plays a concert at The Driskill.*

1934 - *Texas Rangers meet at the hotel to plan the trap that will result in the deaths of noted bank-robbers, Clyde Barrow and Bonnie Parker.*

The hotel's most dramatic change came in 1930 with the opening of the 12-story Driskill Annex, which more than doubled the hotel's total number of rooms. Each room and suite in the tower was the latest word in design and modern conveniences, including a radio connection in each room. It is also interesting to note that in this picture and in many similar images from this time period, for unknown reasons, the tower's orientation is East-West. However, the actual tower faced Brazos Street and ran North-South.

A NEW CENTURY FOR THE DRISKILL

Though the Twentieth Century brought many changes for the capital city of Texas, much of that change was slow in coming. A commuter railroad already connected downtown with an imposing granite dam on the Colorado, and locals and visitors alike were fond of venturing out to Lake McDonald for steamboat excursions on the paddlewheel steamboat Ben Hur. The dam also provided hydroelectric power to the city, which was now lighted with a unique series of tall, "moonlight" towers. But in the Spring of 1900, a massive flood on the Colorado destroyed Austin Dam and the city was plunged back into relative darkness.

In June, 1903, Major Littlefield decided he'd had enough of the hotel business and sold The Driskill to Edward Seeling for $84,000, including all furniture, fixtures and liquors, though operations seem to have been little affected.

As always, the hotel remained a meeting place for the movers and shakers of Texas. In 1908, a bitter feud between factions of the Daughters of the Republic had already become a statewide controversy when the group, led by Mrs. Clara Driscoll, met at the hotel to complete their plan for the preservation for the Alamo. Governor

Thomas M. Campbell came to The Driskill to meet with the group, their plan was given the official sanction of the state, and the Daughters continue to watch over the Alamo to this day.

Over the years, the hotel had been remodeled and redesigned with amazing regularity, though the changes never seemed to do much harm to the building's original design, perhaps because it was so difficult to make any real structural changes. Every alteration made to the hotel's original structure was an exercise in frustration to the teams of architects and builders who came up against the massive beams and fireproof walls and ceilings which resisted all change.

The hotel's most dramatic change occurred in 1930 with the opening of the 12-story Driskill Annex, which brought the hotel's total number of rooms to more than 300. Each room and suite in the tower was the latest word in design and modern conveniences, including a radio connection in every room. Though these new accommodations were stylish, Driskill old-timers generally asked to be lodged in the original building. Every town had a modern hotel, but only Austin had The Driskill.

FRANK HAMER & BONNIE & CLYDE

The Driskill played a role in the annals of Texas law enforcement when a group of Texas Rangers met at the hotel bar to formulate a plan for the capture of bank-robbers Clyde Barrow and Bonnie Parker. Consensus at the meeting was that legendary Ranger Frank Hamer was the man who could bring the outlaws to justice. A long-time patron of The Driskill Bar, Hamer was generally wary of revenge from criminals he'd arrested and always sat with an exit nearby and a view of all entrances. He did not have to fear revenge from Bonnie and Clyde who met their demise in a trap set by Hamer just three months after he took the job dreamed up for him at The Driskill.

> *"Like butterflies, socialites dust the room, flitting in and around this fantastic fairyland garden of the state's powerful and wealthy."*
>
> - Austin American Statesman, 1919

LOW NOTES & HIGH SOCIETY

As the most lavish and comfortable meeting place in Austin, The Driskill was Austin's premier social gathering place and the choice of lodging for visiting artists and dignitaries from across the country. The reputation of The Driskill traveled far, and became one of the chief reasons the nearby Millet Opera House and Hancock Theater could book the country's finest actors and singers. Stars of the day such as Edwin Booth, Frederick Ward and Stuart Robson and the famed Sarah Bernhardt all called The Driskill home while starring in thrilling plays, musicals and operas such as Quo Vadis and the Prisoner of Zenda.

By the twenties, the hotel had already hosted thirty years of University of Texas homecoming balls and numerous other university functions. Looking back at countless newspaper clippings and fading programs, it seems as though every group in town held their meetings and celebrations at the hotel. The Austin Rotary Club met there weekly for fifty-six years from 1913 to 1969.

The Town and Gown Club - whose membership was comprised of one-half University of Texas professors and one-half Austinites with no University affiliation - met at The Driskill on every other Thursday night from 1902 to 1964. Their discussions were dedicated to "free inquiry," no matter the political bent of their speakers, among whom were the three great old men of Texas letters, J. Frank Dobie, Walter Prescott Webb and Roy Bedichek.

Not to be outdone, women's social, political and charitable groups, including the Women's Parliament, the Girl's Settlement Club and the Elizabeth Ney Delphian Chapter, all met regularly at the hotel.

One of the most talked about events of Austin society may have been the 1953 formal dinner at The Driskill hosted and paid for by ranch-and-oil widow Mrs. H.O. Davenport. Inviting the usual Austin collection of powerful politicians and esteemed professors, Mrs. Davenport made certain that J. Mason Brewer, professor at the all-black Huston Tillotson College was also present. That Brewer was a noted scholar and had been published by the University of Texas Press was of less importance than the simple fact that he was black, and that Mrs. Davenport's dinner was the first integrated social function in Austin.

Unwilling to risk alienating any of their constituency, elected officials stayed away by the droves, but a crowd of 150 was on hand when master of ceremonies J. Frank Dobie suggested that their hostess should say a few words.

"I just figgered this situation had gone on long enough, and no one was going to do anything about it," Mrs. Davenport said to the crowd. "I didn't owe nobody nuthin' and nobody owed me. Never had a gigolo. I ain't never given a man a key to my apartment. So I am free to do as I please, and this is what I decided to do."

From that point on, Austin would look forward to a future of equal treatment instead of backward to a time of senseless segregation.

THE HEADLINERS & CITADEL CLUB

In the mid-fifties, just as the old Driskill drug store was about to close, a group of Austin writers, editors and politicians decided they needed a place in downtown Austin to convene and discuss the business of the day. At the time in Austin, you could only purchase a mixed drink at private clubs, so one of their goals may have been to create a watering hole closer than the Austin Golf Club on Riverside Drive.

On April 11, 1955, the remodeled drug store space had a grand opening as the Headliners Club. The crowd of 600 that evening included Hollywood actors Greer Garson and Dana Andrews (which was not an unusually star-studded night as The Driskill frequently played host to celebrities, including Gregory Peck, Carol Burnet and the Duke himself, John Wayne).

So private was the Headliners that each of the members had his own key to open the club's always-locked front door. When the Headliners Club relocated to new quarters a decade later, members still loyal to The Driskill refused to depart the home field and opened the new Citadel Club.

Also playing its part in the history of Texas, the Citadel Club opened on November 20, 1966, with members dealing with questions of politics, Texas arts and literature, and the conservation of Texas natural resources and wildlife.

In 1981, state representative Anita Hill was turned away from the club, which had restricted its facilities during lunch-time hours to men only. The resulting surge of support for women's rights resolved that situation when the Texas House passed a resolution banning any member of the body from attending public or private places that denied access to any member of the House. As a result, in October 1982, full membership privileges to the Citadel Club were granted to women.

STANLEY WALKER - R.I.P.

"For my taste, the world's finest barroom was in the old Driskill Hotel. Better than the Waldorf-Astoria bar on the Plaza in New York? Yes, I still think so. The odor was enough to quicken the spirit - a blend of hard liquors and beer and a gentle haze of cigar smoke. The people were in every way exciting: touring actors (Maurice Barrymore once drank at this bar), remarkable windbags who passed for statesman (United States Senator Joseph Weldon Bailey came in sometimes), bankers with heavy chains across their vests, cattle barons from west Texas and the brush country, solid and heavy-lidded Texas Rangers, important newspaper editors, and an assortment of promoters, dreamers, and flimflam artists such as infest every capital city. This indeed was the place. Here big deals were consummated, lasting friendships were formed, the science of statecraft was refined, and life itself in every way was made more nearly bearable. And more great men, some drinkers and some abstainers, congregated in the cavernous lobby just off the bar. In one way and another I came to know many of these persons; they were easy to meet, openhearted, gregarious, amusing, far different from the suspicious, tight-lipped, evasive, businesslike Texas politician or tycoon that one encounters today."

- Stanley Walker

A Lampasas boy who spent many years in Manhattan as the editor of the New York Herald-Tribune, Walker celebrated one last great night at the Headliner's bar in 1962, then thanked all present for a wonderful time and announced that he was dying of cancer. The following day, Walker passed away while walking through the fields of his Lampasas Ranch.

STRANGE BEDFELLOWS -
POLITICS & THE DRISKILL

Starting with that first grand inaugural ball of Sul Ross in 1887, The Driskill was at the heart of political power, deal making and celebrations in Texas. The tradition of Driskill gubernatorial inaugurals was continued by Governors O.B. Colquitt; Pa Ferguson; his wife Ma Ferguson, the first woman governor of Texas; William P. Hobby; Dan Moody; and finally by John Connally.

Declining to throw a splashy ball for his inaugural in 1921, Governor-elect Pat M. Neff and his family moved into The Driskill for an extended period where he proceeded to receive visitors from across Texas and around the world

The most spectacular of the inaugural affairs was said to have been Governor Hobby's ball in 1919. With the country in an ebullient mood following the end of the Great War, the ball featured multiple orchestras playing simultaneously from behind forests of ferns and lavish decorations, with the entire scene decorated as a fine European Court.

Even considering these historic occasions, The Driskill's chief role in the politics of Texas was as a meeting place both for those who made the decisions of Texas politics and those who wished to influence those decisions.

Over the decades, Governors strolled arm-in-arm with legislators as they passed through the lobby on the way to a comfortable room in which to write legislation, lobbyists bought countless drinks in The Driskill bar for those in power and often for those who merely pretended to have the power.

U.S. Senator Ralph Yarborough's career in politics began with a 1931 meeting at The Driskill which remained for decades, in the Senator's opinion, as the center of Texas politics.

Among the legendary politicians with whom Yarbrough worked at the hotel over the years were: Governor Coke Stevenson - aka "Mr. Texas"; Governor James Allred; Senator and country singer "Pappy" Lee O'Daniel; U.S. Speaker of the House Sam Rayburn; Tennessee Senator Al Gore, Sr.; and, of course, Congressman, Senator, Vice President and, ultimately, President, Lyndon Baines Johnson.

Austin's first television station, KTBC, broadcasts on Channel 7 from the station's studio in The Driskill Hotel on Thanksgiving Day 1952.

**Timeline -
A New Deal & A Great Society**

1934 - *Lyndon Johnson and Lady Bird Taylor have their first date - breakfast in The Driskill dining room.*

1937 - *Lyndon Johnson is elected to the U.S. House of Representatives from the Tenth Congressional District.*

1937 - *First lady Eleanor Roosevelt speaks at The Driskill on "The Problems of Youth."*

1946 - *Voters approve bonds to purchase land for Interstate Highway, IH-35.*

1950 - *Austin's population is 132,000.*

1952 - *The hotel is remodeled to enclose the original rotunda, adding air conditioning to the guest rooms and additional space on the upper floors, but forever altering the character of the hotel.*

Thanksgiving Day 1952 - *Austin's first television station, KTBC, broadcasts on Channel 7 from the station's studio in The Driskill Hotel.*

1953 - *Austin's first integrated social function, a formal dinner, is held at The Driskill.*

1955 - *Cactus Pryor becomes program director of KTBC, hosting a live 30-minute variety show from a second floor studio in The Driskill.*

above, l to r - Charles E. Green, Tom Green, Elizabeth Thomas Booth,
Brown Booth, and Dr. Oliver Suehs at The Headliners Club, c. unknown.

THE PRESIDENT & THE LADY

The Driskill has served as the local address for a number of U.S. Presidents and first ladies, but Austin's grand dame hotel was much more than just an address to Lyndon Baines Johnson, for many of the most significant events of Johnson's life occurred in his favorite hotel.

In 1934, congressional aide Lyndon Johnson whispered an invitation to breakfast at The Driskill dining room to recent University of Texas graduate Lady Bird Taylor. Intrigued by this brash young man, Lady Bird (her nickname since childhood) met young Lyndon at The Driskill, where -among other things - he told her he'd made an acquaintance with Franklin Roosevelt and that he wanted to do big things. The date continued through the entire day, and by sunset, Lyndon said he wanted to marry her. "You must be joking!" Lady Bird told him. Apparently he was not. Ten weeks later, they were married.

After election to the House of Representatives in 1937, Johnson set his political career into high gear with a 1941 meeting at The Driskill, conferring with trusted young advisors J.J. Jake Pickle and John Connally on a decision to run for the U.S. Senate. Though Lyndon was narrowly defeated in the race by W. Lee "Pappy" O'Daniel, Lyndon fared better in his next attempt at the Senate. In 1948, LBJ awaited the results of his U.S. Senate primary run-off at The Driskill with a party in the Maximillian Room, which featured dancing until midnight. The dancing, as it turned out, was over long before the election as Lyndon's victory over Governor Coke Stevenson was not decided until the arrival of late - and much-questioned - results from the infamous Box 13 from Jim Wells County .

In the 1960 presidential election, The Driskill served as the Austin location of the famed "Austin-to-Boston" live telecast between John F. Kennedy and his running mate, Senate Majority Leader Lyndon B. Johnson. The Driskill also served as Johnson's election night headquarters as he awaited the results at his command post in the Jim Hogg Suite on the Mezzanine level. In every public space of the hotel and in the new Headliners Club, the crowds were packed like sardines, partying to celebrate the final word of victory. At three a.m., it was announced that the race was still too close to call. Retiring to his suite on the fourth floor, Lyndon tried to sleep and did not get the word that the Kennedy-Johnson ticket had been victorious until well into the next day.

Four years later - November 3, 1964 - with JFK having been felled in Dallas and Johnson now the President, 200 security officers were present at the Municipal Auditorium and The Driskill as the President of the United States once again came home to await the results of his reelection campaign. Notching a quick and sweeping victory this time, LBJ and his family and friends watched the returns of his re-election at his favorite hotel - The Driskill.

During both of Johnson's terms, whenever the President was in Texas, The Driskill played host to the White House Press Corps. Business and political negotiations took place in The Driskill bar, in the dining room, the lobby, in the hotel's barbershop where Lyndon always said, "don't cut my hair too short," and, of course, in the Jim Hogg and Presidential suites where Lyndon played host to all.

For five and one half years, The Driskill was the center of the greatest show on earth - American politics. After Johnson declined to run again in 1968 and returned to his ranch in Johnson City, he was not the only one diminished by the sad end of a great and long-lasting legacy, for The Driskill's influence faded quickly, too.

In the Fall of 1969, unable to deal with the precipitous drop in business and a world which seemed to be leaving the stately old hotel behind - the owners of The Driskill put all its properties up for auction, all that is, except for the furnishings of the Presidential Suite.

SAVED FROM THE WRECKING BALL

In 1969, after financing fell through for a major addition to the hotel, The Driskill was closed and slated for demolition. Outraged at the possibility of this tragic loss, local citizens enlisted in a preservation battle led by the Heritage Society of Austin. Raising $900,000 in shares at one dollar per share, The Driskill was saved from destruction and within a year was dedicated as a state and federal historic landmark.

Within two years, the entire investment made by the citizens of Austin was fully repaid with interest and a bright new future for The Driskill was at hand.

On February 10, 1973, The Driskill's grand re-opening gala was called a spectacular success, with twelve hundred guests in attendance, including every Texas Governor from the past 20 years and descendants of every governor since the hotel's opening.

Another ownership change took place in 1983 when Lincoln Hotels purchased The Driskill and launched a $4.5 million renovation with the goal of upgrading service and hospitality while restoring The Driskill to its 1886 condition. Among the changes and restorations was the reopening of the dramatic, arched Brazos Street entrance with hotel guests once again entering through the original multi-columned lobby.

NOTABLE GUESTS

Louis Armstrong	President Bill Clinton	Larry L. King	Burt Reynolds
Count Basie	The Doobie Brothers	Taj Mahal	Bonnnie Raitt
Sandra Bullock	Robert Duvall	Delbert McClinton	William Shatner
President George W. Bush	Amelia Earhart	Willie Nelson	Paul Simon
Carol Burnett	Rev. Billy Graham	Sandra Day O'Connor	Sissy Spacek
Greer Garson	Horton Foote	Fess Parker	Lily Tomlin
Van Cliburn	Dennis Hopper	Dolly Parton	Jerry Jeff Walker
Walter Cronkite	Michael Jordan	Gregory Peck	John Wayne
The Dixie Chicks	Tommy Lee Jones	Dan Rather	

opposite page - The L.B. Johnson family and friends watching the presidential election returns in the Jim Hogg Suite, c. 1960.
this page - Gregory Peck and his wife, Veronique Passani, c. 1964.

THE DRISKILL TODAY

Having seen the dawn of two new centuries, The Driskill stands today more than ever as the fully realized dream of Jesse Lincoln Driskill. A great hotel for a great American city, despite all its changes and improvements, the hotel would still bring a familiar smile to the old Colonel.

Built so solidly that she almost defies change - in almost 120 years, The Driskill has seen hardly a door sag - the original concrete and iron sheeting used as fire-proofing has meant that even small alterations must be well-considered. The hotel's most recent renovation and restoration, overseen by Managing Director Jeffrey Trigger, has been a work of wide scope and intricate detail. From the columns of the mezzanine, which have once again been painted and marbleized using turkey feathers as brushes in the style of the 1880s, to the reworking of every room and suite - The Driskill has regained its place as the most gracious of Texas hotels.

As in days of old, the soaring arched entrances on Brazos and Sixth Street again welcome guests to the hotel. Inside the tall, elegant lobby, visitors' eyes wander from the hand-laid marble floor to the elaborately detailed ceiling, and to original artwork and period furnishing which seem to invite you to sit and enjoy life at a proper pace. Looking as if it has been there from day one, the lobby's stained glass inverted dome was custom-made by Stanton Glass Studio in 1999.

In the timeless Driskill Bar on the main floor of the annex, cowboy boots and couture mingle day and night. At the octagonal bar, around the 10-foot piano, or well-seated in over-stuffed leather sofas, Texans and Texas visitors alike gather to discuss the worlds of politics, art, and society. As in days of old, The Driskill continues to play host to a wide range of social, business and political events, including recurring standouts like the Austin Film Festival, the Texas Medal of Arts Awards, the Seton Gala and the Hill Country Wine and Food Festival.

Service, comfort and hospitality are at an all time high at The Driskill, as are the hotel's four-star, four-diamond ratings. Both the recently renovated 1886 Café and Bakery and the elegant Driskill Grill help bring together the traditions and innovation that were key to Colonel Driskill's dream. The reputation of The Driskill Grill brings visitors from far and wide to sample the ever-inventive cuisine of Chef David Bull, who has received a string of five-star ratings to go with what is frequently called the finest food in Austin.

Understanding the demands of busy travelers has long been a Driskill trademark, which is why this historic hotel now offers such high-tech amenities as a Governor's Boardroom with state-of-the-art audiovisual and computer capabilities, a high-tech Executive Business Center, and a fitness studio with everything from private steam rooms to elliptical gliders and stair steppers with their own flat-screen televisions.

At the end of their day, Driskill guests retreat to one of 188 accommodations, each of them individually designed and decorated. Whether staying in the hotel's traditional guest rooms decorated in the color palate of the Texas Hill Country, or in the historic guest rooms with soaring ceilings and custom wrought iron beds, the experience will be as unique as every room in the hotel. Among the hotel's most favored accommodations, the four-room Cattle Baron's Suite is the ultimate in old-world comfort, while the Renaissance Bridal Suite continues to fulfill the bridal fantasies of countless newlyweds.

Whether dining, socializing, doing business or retreating from the hustle and bustle of the modern world, the experience of The Driskill is not easily forgotten. To know her is to love her, and that is exactly what Austinites and Austin visitors will continue to do for years to come.

1991 - *The band Concrete Blonde records their hit song, "Ghost of a Texas Ladies Man" about The Driskill Hotel.*

1995 - *Great American Life Insurance purchases The Driskill and begins a massive restoration.*

1999 - *President Bill Clinton stays at The Driskill.*

1999 - *Austin's population is 630,000.*

December 31, 1999 - *The Driskill celebrates a $30 million renovation with a grand millennium celebration benefiting local charities.*

2001 - *President-elect George W. Bush leases The Driskill Ballroom and Mezzanine for two weeks for cabinet selection meetings.*

2003 - *Chef David Bull is named as One of America's Best Young Chefs by Food and Wine Magazine.*

2005 - *The Driskill Hotel named Travel & Leisure Top 500 Hotels in The World and named to the Conde Nast Traveler Gold List.*

2005 - *Lowe Enterprises Investors acquires The Driskill, and the hotel becomes part of Destination Hotels & Resorts.*

opposite page - The Renaissance Bridal Suite.
this page, top - The Driskill Bar, bottom - The Cattle Baron's Suite.

about the chef

DAVID J. BULL ~ THE YOUNG CHEF IN THE OLD HOTEL

David J. Bull
Executive Chef

THE RAPID RISE IN THE DRISKILL'S LOCAL AND NATIONAL CULINARY REPUTATION is a tribute to the extraordinary talents of the hotel's Executive Chef, David J.Bull. Though just 28 years old when he was named by Food and Wine Magazine as one of the Best New Chefs in America, David Bull is no newcomer to restaurant kitchens.

As a child in upstate New York, young David Bull was a member of a multi-generational restaurant family. "My grandparents owned an Italian restaurant," he says, "and I went to work every day after school — peeling garlic and making manicotti. I owe alot of who I am to that experience. I will never forget those times shared with my grandparents and family."

Two weeks out of high school and just 17 years old, Bull began a twenty-one-month course of study at the prestigious CIA — the Culinary Institute of America. Graduating at age 19, he applied to several five star/five diamond restaurants and was hired by the Mansion on Turtle Creek in Dallas — long considered one of America's top restaurants. Joining forty-two other cooks in the Mansion kitchen, David was promoted in just two years to Sous Chef, then at age 23 to Executive Sous Chef.

When the Mansion's Managing Director Jeffrey Trigger came to Austin to revive The Driskill Hotel, he invited David Bull and a dozen other experienced Mansion colleagues to join him.

As part of a hotel, The Driskill Grill enjoys privileges that stand-alone restaurants may not have. "It is a great luxury to have an infrastructure already in place," says Bull. "We already have our engineering, our housekeeping and our laundry taken care of. And our accolades are extended not only to the Austin community, but also to out-of-town guests staying in the hotel. The hotel draws guests into the restaurant, and vice-versa, it works in great harmony."

The goal of creating the ultimate experience in every aspect of the hotel meant that Bull and his team would have to build a culinary reputation for fine cuisine while also fulfilling the many other important restaurant and catering demands of a great hotel. It did not take long for the local food writers to take note. By 2003, The Driskill Grill had been named the No. 1 restaurant in Austin, an outstanding accomplishment in a city known for its many great restaurants.

The Driskill Hotel's Culinary Staff continually strives to provide innovative and dynamic cuisine. Left to right - Banquet Sous Chef Cesar Gallegos, Assistant Pastry Chef Kim Ruiz, Banquet Chef Saul Revuelta, Sous Chef Alberto Gutierrez, Sous Chef Scott Shoyer, Café Lead Christopher Jewett, Sous Chef Tien Ho, Executive Sous Chef Josh Watkins, Executive Chef David J. Bull.

Three years of renovation provided many new opportunities in the culinary department. Chef Bull remarks, "We started from scratch and began with the systems, organization, physical layout and eventually the hardware. It really was a challenge but it was also a fantastic process. We were able to create a completely new dining experience that continues to be colored by history and tradition. It was the opportunity of a lifetime for me; the culinary staff provided a talented group of people all focused on the same objective—to create wonderful cuisine that allows our guests to enjoy a complete experience of the finest cuisine, service and ambiance in Austin. We've all grown together and we're so proud to be able to look back and see all the progress we've made in these last few years."

High Praise from the Magazine of Texas

From a salad of microgreens and sweet Ruby Red grapefruit sections (with St. André cheese and a fabulous vanilla-vodka vinaigrette) to a sophisticated-but-fun dessert of the lightest peanut butter nougat between homemade graham crackers with a dab of caramel sauce. We ran out of oohs and aahs. In between came a duo of perfect little lamb chops and lamb ossobuco (well-paired with a tangy Jerusalem artichoke purée)...The luxurious chandelier-lit room defines propriety, but the well-trained servers are all friendly smiles. The hours flew by.

— TEXAS MONTHLY MAGAZINE, PATRICIA SHARP

Though he is kept busy by a constant progression of charity events, festivals and cooking demonstrations, Bull never lets his attention wander too far from The Driskill Grill, where every dish is considered to be a reflection of himself and his staff.

"If one component of one dish is off or not perfect, I consider it to be a bad night. You can never become complacent with the dishes you create, and you can never sacrifice the quality or integrity of a dish, ever. If we aren't blown away, excited, or inspired by the dishes we serve, then we haven't done our job."

about the recipes

WHETHER INSPIRED BY THE UNIQUE OFFERINGS OF THE DRISKILL GRILL, the popular classics of the 1886 Café & Bakery, or the special event offerings from the catering department and the hotel's banquet kitchen, the recipes in this book have been created to give the reader an opportunity to prepare food at home that is both simple and sophisticated. That underlying principle of simplicity, premium ingredients, and an overall feeling of comfort with these dishes may soon make them favorites in your home.

From Sunday brunch to a romantic dinner for two, we have taken the essence of what The Driskill offers on a daily basis and created recipes that are easy to duplicate and that won't require you to spend all day in the kitchen. When you can't make it to The Driskill for an important family gathering or special event, just select a few of the recipes from Austin's grande dame of hospitality and cook until your heart is full and your taste buds content.

So without further adieu, bon appetit y'all!

{ TEN GUIDELINES FOR GREAT CUISINE }
by Chef David J. Bull

{1} SEASON EVERYTHING

To obtain the best results, every item must be seasoned properly. The salad, the vinaigrette, the protein, every component must have the perfect level of seasoning.

{2} KNOW YOUR OUTCOME

Know exactly what you want to achieve before you start cooking, including the combinations of flavors you wish to develop and how you want the food to taste and look.

{3} TASTE, TASTE, AND TASTE AGAIN

Taste your ingredients before and after cooking, and before and after seasoning. Training your taste buds to the natural flavors of food allows you to create different taste combinations in your mind before you step into the kitchen.

{4} UNDERSTAND LEVELS OF FLAVOR

A dish can have one or many levels of flavor. A peanut butter and jelly sandwich, for instance, has two levels — peanut butter, which can be salty and bitter, and jelly, which is sweet. A common mistake is to have too many flavors and too many combinations. Stick to basic combinations and minimal levels of flavor and your end results will be more appetizing.

{5} UTILIZE THE ESSENTIAL FLAVORS

There are four traditional categories of food flavors: salty, bitter, sweet, and sour. The difference between a good meal and a great meal is the ability to combine these elements successfully. Understanding simple but successful combinations of flavors is the key to creating an incredible dining experience.

{6} TEXTURE

After flavor, texture is the next most important aspect of great food. By utilizing the sense of touch, texture expands the way we experience our food, and can be used in combinations — understanding the way food "feels" is crucial to great cuisine.

{7} TEMPERATURE

The combination of cold, hot or room temperature ingredients can make or break a particular dish in the same way as combining flavors. Attention to temperature differences from dish to dish can greatly enhance the overall dining experience.

{8} FOLLOWING RECIPES

While developing your cooking skills, it's important to follow recipes as closely as possible. But once you've developed your chops — so to speak — don't be afraid of mistakes or your own creativity. Knowing your ingredients and understanding their role in a particular dish frees you to create your own dishes.

{9} PRESENTATION

Though flavor always comes first, the way your food looks has a great effect on how it will taste. The visual aspect of food relies upon a focal point and proper use of lines and color. Use the natural beauty of your ingredients' shapes and sizes to maximum visual advantage.

{10} BE CREATIVE AND HAVE FUN

Don't be afraid to experiment with new ingredients or innovative presentation. Have fun with the creation of your food, and don't forget to taste!

BREAKFAST IN BED
The Heritage Suite

THE MENU

Cinnamon Coffee Cake French Toast with Fig Jam

Mini Croissants with Pecan Butter

Mixed Berry Parfait with Chantilly Cream

With its soaring ceiling, luxurious bed and a beautiful private balcony, the Heritage Suite is one of the hotel's most romantic accommodations. One of only four original guest chambers that had it's own private bath, the suite now has both a sauna shower and a jacuzzi tub for two, just the thing to put you in the mood for a romantic breakfast in bed.

If you're in a similar mood at home, Cinnamon Coffee Cake French Toast makes for a perfect breakfast in your own bed. Prepare the coffee cake on Saturday morning and use the leftovers for the French toast at Sunday breakfast. You might even stay in bed for lunch.

CINNAMON COFFEE CAKE FRENCH TOAST
WITH FIG JAM

Serves 2 | *Breakfast In Bed*

For the Assembly

Dip each coffee cake slice into the batter. Grill the battered coffee cake slices on a preheated griddle or cast iron pan until golden brown and crisp on both sides. On four large dinner plates arrange two pieces of the Coffee Cake French Toast shingled on top of one another. Spoon or ladle one-two tablespoons of fig jam over the top of the slices and garnish with powdered sugar and cinnamon sticks.

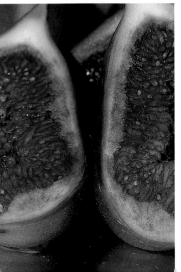

THE RECIPE

10 inch round Coffee cake
1 cup cinnamon French toast batter
1 cup Fig jam
2 each Cinnamon sticks for garnish
Powdered sugar for garnish

For the Streusel Topping

1 cup Brown sugar
6 tablespoons Sugar
4 teaspoons Cinnamon
1½ cups Cake flour
12 tablespoons Butter, unsalted, softened

Place all of the above ingredients into a mixer with the paddle attachment and mix until the ingredients are coarse and crumbly.

For the Coffee Cake Batter

9 each Large eggs
1⅓ cups Sour cream
3 teaspoons Vanilla extract
4¼ cups Cake flour
2 cups Sugar
1 teaspoon Baking soda
1 teaspoon Baking powder
½ teaspoon Salt
1¾ cup Butter, softened

Combine the eggs, ¼ of the sour cream and vanilla extract in a bowl and mix thoroughly. Set aside. Combine the cake flour, sugar, baking soda, baking powder and salt in a mixer and mix thoroughly. Add remaining ¾ of the sour cream and butter to the dry ingredients and mix on low until moistened. Beat on medium speed for 1½ minutes. Scrape down the sides of the bowl and while mixing add the egg-sour cream mixture in three even batches. Line the bottom of a 10-inch round cake pan or coffee cake pan with parchment paper and grease all sides very well. Pour ½ of the cake batter in and smooth out with an offset spatula. Sprinkle ½ of the crumb streusel topping over the surface of the batter. Pour the remaining cake batter in and top the batter with the remaining crumb streusel topping. Bake in a preheated 350-degree oven for 35-45 minutes or until a toothpick comes out clean and the cake springs back when touched.

For the French Toast Batter

4 each Whole eggs
2 ounces Whole milk
1 teaspoon Cinnamon
1 teaspoon Grand Marnier or orange liqueur

In a stainless steel bowl, using a wire whisk, whip all ingredients together. Reserve to batter the coffee cake.

For the Fig Jam

10 each Black mission figs, stem removed, rough chopped
5 teaspoons Red wine vinegar
4 teaspoons Sugar

Combine all ingredients into a saucepot and bring to a boil over medium heat. Turn down to low heat and simmer for 3-5 minutes. Place mixture into a blender and puree until smooth.

THE RECIPE

24 each Mini croissants
¾ cup Pecan butter

For the Mini Croissants

3⅓ cups Bread flour
¼ cup Sugar
1½ teaspoons Salt
1 tablespoon Dry active yeast
1½ cups Milk
½ cup Butter, unsalted, softened

Preheat oven to 350 degrees. Combine the bread flour, sugar, salt and dry yeast together in a mixer for 5 minutes, or until well incorporated. Add the milk and mix for 5 minutes or until the dough pulls from the sides of the bowl. Let the dough rest in the refrigerator, covered, for one hour. Roll out the dough into an 11-inch thick square. Spread the soft butter over ⅔ of the dough. Fold ⅓ of the dough over the middle and then the remaining ⅓ over both previous folds as though folding a letter. Refrigerate for 30 minutes. Repeat the letter folds 3 more times, resting for 30 minutes in the refrigerator in between each turn, creating several layers of butter. Then divide and cut the dough into four equal parts. Roll the dough to ⅛ of an inch thickness and cut into long triangles measuring 6-7 inches long. You should get six triangles from each quarter of dough. Starting with the widest end roll the dough away from yourself ending at the point of the triangle, creating a croissant shape. Fold the ends together and set in a warm place to proof for 1 hour or until the croissants double in size. Mix the eggs with the water to form an egg wash and lightly brush the egg wash on the croissants covering all sides. Bake in a preheated 350-degree oven for 20-25 minutes or until they are golden brown.

For the Egg Wash

3 each Eggs
6 tablespoons Water

Mix the eggs with the water to form an egg wash.

For the Pecan Butter

½ cup Pecan halves
2 each Egg whites, whipped
½ cup Sugar
8 ounces Whole butter, room temperature

Preheat oven to 300 degrees. Toss the pecan halves with the whipped egg whites and combine with the sugar. Spread the pecans evenly on a sheet pan and bake in a preheated 300-degree oven for 15-20 minutes or until the pecans are well toasted. Be sure to stir the pecans every 3-5 minutes for even toasting. Allow the pecans to cool and, using a food processor, chop the pecans, pulsing briefly until they are small and even pieces. Combine the chopped pecans with the room temperature butter and mix well. Using parchment paper, place the butter into the center of the paper. Fold the paper over the butter and mold the butter into a long square or shape desired. Place into the refrigerator until completely chilled and slice into small blocks.

MINI CROISSANTS WITH PECAN BUTTER

Serves 2 | *Breakfast In Bed*

For the Assembly

Set the croissants onto a small plate and place the pecan butter next to the croissants.

MIXED BERRY PARFAIT WITH CHANTILLY CREAM

Serves 2 | *Breakfast In Bed*

For the Assembly

In two parfait glasses, place the angel food cake on the bottom and layer the mixed berries and the chantilly cream alternately until the glass is full. Top the parfait with a dollop of the chantilly cream and garnish with powdered sugar and a sprig of mint.

THE RECIPE

1 pint Mixed berries
10 inch round Angel food cake
6 ounces Chantilly cream
Mint sprigs for garnish
Powdered sugar for garnish

For the Angel Food Cake

4 ounces Cake flour
12 ounces Sugar
1 teaspoon Cream of tartar
12 each Egg whites
2 teaspoons Vanilla extract
2 teaspoons Lemon juice

Sift the cake flour with half of the sugar. Combine the other half of the sugar and the cream of tartar together. Place the egg whites into a bowl and using a mixer with the whip attachment, whip the egg whites on medium-high speed. As the egg whites are whipping, slowly add the sugar and cream of tartar mixture. Continue whipping until the egg whites reach stiff peaks. In a large mixing bowl, gently fold together the whipped egg whites and the cake flour/sugar mixture until well combined. Line a 10-inch round cake pan or angel food cake pan with parchment paper. Add the angel food cake mix to pan and bake in a preheated 325-degree oven for 55 minutes. Invert the cake upside down on a cooling rack and allow to completely cool. Slice the cake across in three equal portions creating three large discs all the same thickness. Using a 3-inch biscuit cutter cut the cake into small rounds and reserve for assembly.

For the Chantilly Cream

1 cup Heavy whipping cream
3 teaspoons Sugar
¼ teaspoon Vanilla extract

Place all of the ingredients into a bowl and, using a mixer with a whip attachment, whip the cream mixture until it forms medium peaks or resembles whipped cream.

The Heritage Suite

The Heritage Suite, one of the original suites, was home to the Heritage Society of Austin. This altruistic organization rallied Austin's citizens and raised funds to save The Driskill from certain demolition in 1969. This exquisite suite is named in their honor.

SUNDAY BRUNCH
The 1886 Café & Bakery

THE MENU

Buttermilk Biscuits with Apricot Marmalade

Poached Eggs with Ham, Brie Cheese, and Horseradish Hollandaise

Mustard & Sage Crusted Pork Loin with Red Applesauce

Grilled Asparagus with Shaved Parmesan and Balsamic Syrup

Citrus fruit Salad with Toasted Almonds and Vanilla Yogurt

Apple Crunch Granola

Silver Dollar Ginger Snap-Huckleberry Pancakes

Peach Cobbler with Cornmeal Struesal and Vanilla Ice Cream

WITH A VITAL LOCATION LOOKING OUT ON SIXTH STREET and spilling out across the south entrance of the hotel, the space now occupied by the 1886 Café & Bakery has served as a telegraph office, a billiard and pool hall, the 1886 Lunchroom, and finally as a full-service cafe serving everything from cappuccino and an elegant Sunday Brunch to a glass of fine wine with a late-evening snack.

These recipes are chosen both because they represent the old-world heritage of The Driskill and because they are perfect for a great Sunday brunch. The mustard and sage crusted pork loin and buttermilk biscuits are Southern classics, the unique presentations and sophistication will be the highlight of any afternoon.

BUTTERMILK BISCUITS WITH APRICOT MARMALADE

Serves 8 | *Sunday Brunch*

For the Assembly

Place the warm biscuits in a small cloth-lined basket and place the apricot marmalade in small ramekins.

THE RECIPE

12-16 each Buttermilk biscuits
2 cups Apricot marmalade

For the Buttermilk Biscuits

1¼ cups Bread flour
¾ cup Cake flour
⅓ cup Sugar
1½ tablespoons Baking powder
½ teaspoon Salt
½ cup unsalted Butter, cubed
½ cup Shortening
¼ cup Eggs
2 cups Buttermilk
1 cup All purpose flour

Preheat oven to 350 degrees and line a baking sheet with parchment paper. Sift together the bread flour, cake flour, sugar, baking powder and salt into a pile on a clean work surface. Cut in the cubed butter and gently mix in the shortening. Create a well in the center of the mixture. Mix together the eggs and the buttermilk. Slowly add the egg-buttermilk mixture into the flour and knead the dough until it can form a ball. Sprinkle the dough and the work surface with all purpose flour then roll out the dough to ¼ - ½ inch thick. Cut the dough into round biscuits and place together on the parchment-lined baking sheet. Bake in a pre-heated 350 degree oven for 15-18 minutes or until golden brown.

For the Apricot Marmalade

1 cup White wine vinegar
1¼ cup White sugar
4 each Oranges, zest only
3 each Lemons, zest only
8 each Apricots, chopped, pits and stems removed

Place all ingredients into a medium-size saucepot over medium heat and bring to a boil. Reduce to a simmer and allow to cook for 18-25 minutes or until it becomes slightly thick. Place into a blender and puree until smooth. Refrigerate until completely cold and serve.

8 each Poached eggs
8 slices Smoked quality ham (12 ounces)
8 slices Brie cheese (12 ounces)
1 cup Horseradish hollandaise
4 each English muffins, toasted

For the Poached Eggs

8 each Large eggs
½ cup White wine vinegar
1 quart (4 cups) Water

Using a medium-size saucepot, mix the vinegar and the water together. Bring the water up to 200 degrees or just below a boil. Stir the water in circles causing a whirlpool effect and crack and drop one egg at a time into the water. Cook six eggs at a time. Cook until desired doneness and serve.

For the Horseradish Hollandaise

4 each Egg yolks
1 each Lemon, juiced
2-3 cups Clarified butter warmed to 110 degrees
½ - 1 tablespoon Horseradish, prepared
Tabasco to taste
Worcestershire to taste
Salt to taste
Water as needed

Fill a medium-sized saucepot with water and place on a stove. Bring the water to a boil and turn down to a simmer. Place the egg yolks, lemon juice and 2-3 tablespoons of warm water into a large stainless steel bowl. Using a wire whip, whip the eggs vigorously over the hot water bath. While whipping constantly, cook the eggs until they form soft-medium ribbons. Remove the egg mixture from the heat and secure in place. Using a ladle and, whipping constantly, add the warm clarified butter to the egg mixture 2 ounces at a time until the butter is all incorporated. Add the horseradish and taste. Season the hollandaise with Tabasco, Worcestershire and salt to taste. Reserve in a warm place until assembly.

POACHED EGGS WITH HAM, BRIE CHEESE, AND HORSERADISH HOLLANDAISE

Serves 8 | *Sunday Brunch*

For the Assembly

Top each toasted English muffin with sliced ham and then with the brie cheese. Place into a preheated 300-degree oven until the ham is hot and the cheese is melted. Place the poached eggs onto each muffin and top with the horseradish hollandaise. Serve immediately.

MUSTARD AND SAGE CRUSTED PORK LOIN WITH ROASTED RED APPLESAUCE

Serves 8 | *Sunday Brunch*

For the Assembly

Place the sliced pork loins slightly overlapping each other onto a platter. Fill the roasted red apples with the red applesauce. Garnish with fried sage leaves.

THE RECIPE

1 each Mustard and sage crusted pork loin
10 ounces Roasted red applesauce
6 each Roasted red apples
Fried sage leaves for garnish

For the Mustard and Sage Crusted Pork Loin

1 each , 2-3 pound Pork loin, cleaned, silver skin and fat removed
Salt to taste
Pepper to taste
¼ cup Canola oil
¾ cup Dijon mustard
¾ cup Whole grain mustard
5 tablespoons Sage, finely chopped
4 cups Bread crumbs

Preheat oven to 375 degrees. Season the pork loin with salt and pepper on all sides. In a large skillet over high heat add the canola oil and sear the pork loin on all sides until it becomes golden brown and crisp. Place the pork loin on a baker's rack on a sheet pan and place into a preheated 375-degree oven and cook for 18-30 minutes or until desired doneness is reached. Mix the Dijon mustard and the whole grain mustard together. Mix the chopped sage and the bread crumbs together. Spread the mustard mix generously over the top, sides and ends of the pork loin creating an even coating of mustard. Cover the mustard with the sage breadcrumbs and lightly pack. Place the crusted pork loin into a preheated 375-degree oven for 8-10 minutes or until the crust is golden brown. Remove the pork from the oven and allow it to rest for 10 minutes.
Slice the pork into desired thickness and serve.

For the Red Applesauce

5 each Red apples, peeled, stem, seeds and core removed, large diced
¼ cup Apple cider vinegar
½ cup Sugar
1 teaspoon Cinnamon
1 cup Apple juice

Add all ingredients into a medium-sized saucepot and bring to a boil over high heat. Turn down to a simmer and cook until the apples are soft or for about 15 minutes. Place the ingredients into a blender and puree until smooth.

For the Roasted Red Apples

6 each Red apples
4 ounces Butter
¼ cup Brown sugar

Preheat oven to 300 degrees. Cut the tops off of each apple being careful to keep the stems attached. Using a melon baller, scoop out the centers of each apple, removing all seeds. Place the butter and the sugar in a saucepan and bring to a boil. Using a brush, glaze the apples and tops on all sides, inside and out. Place the tops on a baking sheet and place the apple bottoms on a separate baking sheet. Bake the tops for 4-6 minutes or until soft, and bake the bottoms for 12-15 minutes or until soft. Fill each baked apple with the red applesauce and place the baked top back on the apple and serve.

GRILLED ASPARAGUS WITH SHAVED PARMESAN AND BALSAMIC SYRUP

Serves 8 | *Sunday Brunch*

For the Assembly

Place the asparagus onto a platter and drizzle the balsamic syrup around and on top of the asparagus, sprinkle with shaved Parmesan cheese.

18 each Asparagus sprigs
½ cup Balsamic syrup
Parmesan cheese for garnish

For the Grilled Asparagus

18 each Asparagus, peeled
Water as needed
Salt to taste

In a large saucepot add the water and season with salt. Bring the water to a boil and blanch the asparagus for 3-5 minutes or until bright green and slightly cooked through. Remove the asparagus from the water and place into an ice bath to shock and to stop the cooking process. Preheat a charcoal, gas or wood-burning grill to medium-high. Place the asparagus on the grill and char slightly. Reserve warm for assembly.

For the Balsamic Syrup

1 cup Balsamic vinegar
½ cup White sugar

Place both ingredients into a saucepot and bring to a boil. Reduce the mixture by half over high heat and allow to completely cool. Reserve for assembly.

THE RECIPE

6 cups Citrus fruit salad
½ cup Toasted almond slivers
2 cups Vanilla yogurt
Mint sprigs for garnish

For the Citrus Fruit Salad

1 cup Red grapes, cleaned and cut in half lengthwise
2 cups Pineapple, peeled, center removed and diced
1 cup Honeydew, peeled and diced
1 cup Cantaloupe, peeled and diced
1 cup Oranges, peeled and sectioned
½ cup Almond slivers, toasted
½ cup Lemon juice

Place all ingredients into a large bowl and mix well.

For the Vanilla Yogurt

1½ cups Yogurt
2 each Vanilla beans, split
1 teaspoon Vanilla extract
3 tablespoons Honey

Place all ingredients into a bowl and mix well.

CITRUS FRUIT SALAD WITH TOASTED ALMONDS AND VANILLA YOGURT

Serves 8 | *Sunday Brunch*

For the Assembly

Mix the citrus fruit salad in a serving bowl and spoon the vanilla yogurt on top. Sprinkle the salad with toasted almond slivers and garnish with mint sprigs.

APPLE CRUNCH GRANOLA

Serves 8 | *Sunday Brunch*

For the Assembly

Place the apple crunch granola into a serving bowl and garnish with sliced strawberries. Serve with cold milk.

6 cups Apple crunch granola
4 cups Cold milk
Sliced strawberries as needed

For the Apple Crunch Granola

1 cup Honey
1 cup Apple juice
1 each Cinnamon stick
6 cups Granola
1 cup Raisins
1 cup Slivered almonds
2 cups Dried apples, diced

Preheat an oven to 300 degrees. Place the apple juice, honey and cinnamon stick into a saucepot and bring to a boil. Remove the cinnamon stick. In a large bowl mix the granola, raisins, almonds and apples together. Pour the hot apple-honey mixture over the granola mix and mix well. Spread the mixture evenly onto a large sheet pan lined with parchment paper and bake in a preheated 300-degree oven for 20-30 minutes turning every 10 minutes, or until golden brown and crisp. Allow to cool and serve.

SILVER DOLLAR GINGER SNAP-HUCKLEBERRY PANCAKES

Serves 8 | *Sunday Brunch*

For the Assembly

On a large platter shingle the silver dollar pancakes in a circular fashion. Top with ground gingersnap cookies, huckleberries and dust with powdered sugar. Serve the warm maple syrup on the side.

THE RECIPE

24 each Silver dollar pancakes
3 tablespoons Powdered sugar
10 ounces Maple syrup, warmed

For the Silver Dollar Ginger Snap-Huckleberry Pancakes

3 cups All purpose flour
2 teaspoons Salt
¾ cup Sugar
1 tablespoon Baking soda
2 tablespoons Baking powder
3 pints Buttermilk
3 ounces Butter, melted
6 each Whole eggs, beaten
2 cups Huckleberries *(may substitute blueberries or blackberries)
10 each Gingersnap cookies, ground

Preheat griddle to 300 degrees. Sift together the flour, salt, sugar, baking soda and baking powder into a large mixing bowl. In a separate bowl, whisk together the buttermilk, eggs and half of the melted butter. Add the wet ingredients to the dry ingredients and combine. Brush the preheated griddle with the remaining melted butter. Drop the batter onto the griddle to form 2- to 3-inch silver dollar pancakes. Add a small amount of huckleberries and ground gingersnap cookies to each pancake. Once the tops begin to bubble, flip and continue cooking until the pancakes are cooked through, about 3-5 minutes. Reserve hot for assembly.

PEACH COBBLER WITH CORNMEAL STREUSEL AND VANILLA ICE CREAM

Serves 8 | *Sunday Brunch*

For the Assembly

Serve the peach cobbler in the cast-iron skillet hot. Using a spoon or serving utensil, scoop the peach cobbler out of the cast-iron skillet and place onto a plate. Top with a scoop of vanilla ice cream and drizzle with caramel sauce.

THE RECIPE

1 each Peach cobbler
3 cups Cornmeal streusel topping
2 pints Vanilla ice cream
6 ounces Caramel sauce

For the Peach Cobbler Filling

7 each Medium fresh peaches, cut into wedges
1 cup Sugar
2 tablespoons Cornstarch
1 tablespoon Cinnamon, ground

Peel and cut up peaches. Place in a bowl. Add sugar, cornstarch, and cinnamon to peaches and toss together. Set aside.

For the Cornmeal Streusel Topping

2 cups + 2 tablespoons All purpose flour
1¾ cups Cornmeal
1¼ cup Sugar
2 tablespoons + ½ tablespoon Baking powder
½ teaspoon Salt
½ teaspoon Baking soda
⅓ cup Butter (unsalted)
1¾ cup Heavy cream
8 cups Peach cobbler filling *(see recipe above)

Preheat oven to 350 degrees. In a mixer with the paddle attachment, combine the all purpose flour, cornmeal, sugar, baking powder, salt, and baking soda. While the mixer is on low speed, slowly add the butter. Mix until it resembles a coarse meal. Add the cream slowly on low speed until well combined. Place the peach cobbler filling into a greased cast-iron skillet. Crumble dough on top of peach filling. Bake for about 20 minutes or until golden brown. Reserve hot for assembly.

For the Caramel Sauce

1¼ cup Sugar
1 tablespoon Water
1-2 tablespoons Heavy cream

Combine water and sugar in a saucepan. Heat on high until sugar begins to caramelize and turn an amber color. Carefully pour heavy cream into the saucepan and stir. Remove from heat and reserve warm until assembly.

For the Vanilla Ice Cream

4 cups Heavy cream
1⅓ cups Sugar
12 each Yolks
2 each Vanilla beans
2 cups Milk

Prepare an ice water bath and set aside. Whisk the yolks and the milk together and set aside. In a pot, bring the heavy cream, sugar, and vanilla beans to a boil. Slowly add the heavy cream mixture to the egg mixture while you whisk it. When combined, place back into pot over low heat and stir constantly until it thickens slightly. Quickly place in ice water bath and stir slowly until cool. Chill for about 2-3 hours. Turn in an ice cream machine until firm but soft. Ice cream will continue to set in the freezer. Freeze for about 2 hours before serving.

1886 Café & Bakery

On October 10, 1899 the Southwestern Telephone Company inaugurated its interstate telephone line at The Driskill. Thousands of people poured into The Driskill to attend the "Grand Blow-out" party celebrating the historic first.

WELCOME

1886
CAFÉ & BAKERY
D

OPEN DAILY 7 A.M. TO MIDNIGHT
FRI. & SAT. 7 A.M. TO 2 A.M.

AUSTIN, TEXAS

HOT SUMMER PICNIC
The Brazos Street Terrace

THE MENU

Ginger-Mint Iced Tea

Grilled Shrimp Salad with Roasted Corn and Jicama

Pickled Pears

Marinated Heirloom Tomatoes

Key Lime Tart with Swiss Meringue

THE DRISKILL TERRACES have always been a great spot for a hot summer day. Before the advent of air conditioning, Austinites were particularly fond of the hotel's natural cooling system which funneled cooler air from the lower floors up through the open rotunda, then down the hallways to the deep-shaded terraces.

Our picnic recipes are a double pleasure, for they require just a few minutes to prepare, while the result is a light, refreshing summer picnic of your own. Just add shade.

GINGER-MINT ICED TEA

Serves 2 | *Hot Summer Picnic*

THE RECIPE

½ gallon Iced tea, freshly brewed
1 cup Fresh mint, loosely packed
1 bulb Ginger, sliced into thin discs
Lemon wedges for garnish
Sugar to taste

Mix all ingredients together and allow to sit
for 4-6 hours. Serve cold over ice and garnish
with lemon wedges. Serve with sugar.

GRILLED SHRIMP SALAD WITH ROASTED CORN AND JICAMA

Serves 2 | *Hot Summer Picnic*

For the Assembly

Place a piece of parchment paper on a large dinner
plate or bowl and place the salad in the center. Place
the shrimp on the side of the salad and garnish with
more pepita seeds, corn kernels and cilantro.

THE RECIPE

4 cups Grilled shrimp salad
½ cup Cilantro lime vinaigrette
Corn kernels, pepita seeds and cilantro sprigs for garnish

For the Grilled Shrimp Salad

10 each U-12 shrimp, peeled and deveined, salt to taste
1 head Romaine lettuce, chopped
½ cup Jicama, julienned
½ cup Cucumber, julienned
½ cup Corn kernels, roasted, reserve 1/2 for garnish
2 tablespoons Pepita seeds, toasted, reserve 1/2 for garnish
½ cup Cilantro-lime vinaigrette

Preheat outdoor grill to 350 degrees. Lay the shrimp side by side in two
rows of five, on a clean flat service. Using two wooden skewers, skewer both
the top and tail ends of both rows of five shrimp. Season with salt to taste
and cook on a preheated 350-degree grill for 2-4 minutes on each side or
until cooked through. Remove the skewers and reserve hot. Using a large
mixing bowl, combine the romaine, jicama, cucumber, corn and pepita
seeds. Toss with the cilantro-lime vinaigrette and season with salt to taste.

For the Cilantro-Lime Vinaigrette

1 cup Cilantro, loosely packed
¼ cup Canola oil
4 each Limes, juiced
Salt to taste

Place all ingredients into a blender and puree until smooth.
Season with salt to taste.

PICKLED PEARS

Serves 2 | *Hot Summer Picnic*

THE RECIPE

5 each Pears, peeled and cut into half moon shapes
1 tablespoon Whole black pepper
4 each Whole arbol chilis
1 cup Rice wine vinegar
1 tablespoon White sugar
1 each Lemon, sliced, seeds removed
1 tablespoon Honey

In a saucepot combine all ingredients, except for the
pears. Bring the mixture to a boil and pour over the
pears in a large bowl. Mix thoroughly and place into
the refrigerator — refrigerate until completely cool.
Allow to marinate for 12-24 hours and serve.

MARINATED HEIRLOOM TOMATOES

Serves 2 | *Hot Summer Picnic*

THE RECIPE

3 cups Assorted heirloom tomatoes, large dice
3 each Shallots, minced
1 tablespoon Parsley, finely chopped
3 tablespoons Extra virgin olive oil
Salt to taste

Mix all ingredients together. Season with salt to taste.
Allow to marinate for at least 2 hours before serving.

KEY LIME TART WITH SWISS MERINGUE

Serves 2 | *Hot Summer Picnic*

THE RECIPE

3 ½ cups Key lime filling
3 cups Graham cracker crust
2 ¾ cups Swiss meringue

For the Key Lime filling

1 ¼ cups Sweetened condensed milk
1 cup Egg yolks
1 cup Lime juice

Combine all the ingredients in a small mixing bowl with the paddle attachment. Mix until well combined and set aside.

For the Graham Cracker crust

1 cup Graham cracker crumbs
1 tablespoon Sugar
⅓ cup Unsalted butter (melted)

Combine all the ingredients in a bowl and mix until the ingredients begin to clump together. Press into six 4-inch, Teflon-coated tart pans and set aside.

For the Swiss Meringue

1 cup Egg whites
1 ⅓ cups Sugar

Combine the egg whites and sugar in a bowl over a double boiler. Slowly stir with a wire whisk for 8-10 minutes or until mixture is heated through and the sugar dissolves. Pour mixture into a mixer using a whisk attachment and whisk until it triples in volume and forms stiff peaks. Use immediately.

For the Assembly

Preheat oven to 350 degrees. Fill the graham cracker crusts with the key lime filling and bake for 18-20 minutes or until it is slightly firm and doesn't stick to fingers when lightly touched. Cool completely, and chill in refrigerator for about 2-3 hours. Remove from tart pans. Place the Swiss Meringue into a piping bag with a star tip. Carefully pipe elongated stars next to each other over the entire surface of the tart. Using a torch, lightly brown the Swiss Meringue and serve.

Ⓓ
The Brazos Street Terrace

It is said that although Texas laws were passed just down the street at the State Capitol, the real wheeling and dealing in Texas politics took place at The Driskill—through the lobbies, in the back rooms, and on the terraces.

TEXAS FEAST
The Crystal Room

In COLONEL DRISKILL'S DAY, the area currently occupied by the hotel's elegant Crystal Room was the hotel's horse stable. After exiting wagons and carriages at the Sixth Street entrance—where the sidewalks were three feet high to accommodate the tall horse-drawn vehicles—the horses were taken around to the north side of the building where the prevailing south breezes would carry any smells away from the hotel. None of that original structure is evident today, but the elegant chandeliers now found in the Crystal Room were originally in The Driskill Ballroom. The recipes of the Texas Feast are also a bit more refined than the food eaten in Colonel Driskill's days on the trail, but they do use indigenous Texas ingredients with a Southwestern flavor. The result is an over-the-top, family-style, kick-up-your-heels Texas feast—the perfect meal before a carriage ride down Congress Avenue.

THE MENU

Poblano Mashed Potatoes

Texas Chop Salad with Smoked Bacon and Bleu Cheese

Yellow Tomato Gazpacho with Jicama Hot Stix

Tortilla Crusted Red Snapper with Orange-Tomatillo Salsa

Blueberry Buckle, Meyer Lemon Sorbet and Chilled Almond Soup

TEXAS CHOP SALAD WITH SMOKED BACON AND BLEU CHEESE

Serves 8 | *Texas Feast*

For the Assembly

Mix the romaine, jicama, smoked bacon, red bell peppers, bleu cheese crumbles and the bleu cheese dressing together in a large mixing bowl and season with salt to taste. Transfer the salad to a serving bowl and top with pepita seeds, cotija cheese, corn tortillas, and plantain chips.

THE RECIPE

3 hearts Romaine lettuce, medium diced
1 each Jicama, peeled, julienne
1 pound Smoked bacon, short julienne, rendered crisp
2 each Red bell peppers, roasted, peeled, small diced
1 cup Bleu cheese crumbles
2 cups Bleu cheese dressing
3 tablespoons Pepita (pumpkin) seeds, toasted and ground
¼ cup Cotija cheese, grated
2 cups Corn tortilla strips
2 cups Plantain chips

For the Bleu Cheese Dressing

1 pound Maytag bleu cheese, crumbled
2 cups Sour cream
5-8 drops Tabasco
½ cup Red wine vinegar
3 each Limes, juiced
Salt to taste

Place the bleu cheese, red wine vinegar, sour cream, Tabasco and lime juice into a food processor and pulse until desired consistency is reached. It should be smooth but chunky. Season with salt to taste.

POBLANO MASHED POTATOES

Serves 8 | *Texas Feast*

For the Assembly

Using a piping bag, pipe or place the potatoes into a large bowl and serve.

THE RECIPE

4 cups Poblano mashed potatoes

For the Poblano Mashed Potatoes

8 each Idaho potatoes, peeled and large diced
Water as needed
Salt to taste
3 cups Heavy cream
½ cup Whole butter
2 each Poblano peppers, roasted, seeded and small diced
Salt to taste

Preheat an oven to 300 degrees. Place the potatoes into a large saucepot and cover with water. Thoroughly season with salt. Bring the water to a boil and turn down heat to medium. Cook the potatoes at a simmer over medium heat until fork tender. Drain the potatoes and place into a preheated 300-degree oven for 5-8 minutes or until dry. Place the cream and butter into a saucepan and bring to a boil. Rice the potatoes into a large boil bowl and pour two-thirds of the hot, heavy cream butter mixture over the potatoes. Mix well and fold in the poblano peppers. Add the rest of the cream butter mixture, if necessary to obtain the right consistency. Season with salt to taste and reserve hot for assembly.

above - A traditional family-style Texas buffet, shown here in the Chisolm Trail Room. Laura Clyde worked in food service at The Driskill, c. 1960.

YELLOW TOMATO GAZPACHO
WITH JICAMA HOT STIX

Serves 8 | *Texas Feast*

For the Assembly

Ladle equal portions of the gazpacho into 8 chilled
soup bowls. Place the jicama hot stix into the soup
bowls and garnish with sprigs of cilantro.

THE RECIPE

8 cups Yellow tomato gazpacho
20-24 each Jicama hot stix
Cilantro sprigs for garnish

For the Yellow Tomato Gazpacho

8 each Yellow tomatoes, core removed and quartered
1-2 each Jalapenos, seeded, minced
2 teaspoons Cilantro, finely chopped
2 cups Cucumber, small diced
2 cups Red onion, finely chopped
4 tablespoons Lime juice
Salt to taste

Place the yellow tomatoes into a blender and puree until
smooth. Place into a mixing bowl and combine with jalapenos,
cilantro, cucumber and red onion. Add the lime juice and
season with salt to taste. Keep cold until service.

For the Jicama Hot Stix

2-4 each Jicama, cut into ¼-inch by 3-inch stix
1 teaspoon Arbol chilis, toasted and ground
1 tablespoon Cilantro, finely chopped
2 tablespoons Lime juice
Salt to taste

In a large bowl combine the jicama, arbol chilies, cilantro
and lime juice and season with salt to taste.

TORTILLA CRUSTED RED SNAPPER
WITH ORANGE-TOMATILLO SALSA

Serves 8 | *Texas Feast*

For the Assembly

Place the crusted snapper onto a serving
platter and spoon or ladle the orange-
tomatillo salsa over the snapper.

8 each Tortilla crusted snapper
2 cups Orange-tomatillo salsa
1 cup Cilantro mayonnaise

For the Tortilla Crusted Red Snapper

4 ounces Canola oil
8 each Red snapper filets, bones removed, skin on
Salt to taste
½ cup Corn tortillas, ground
½ cup Cilantro mayonnaise

Preheat oven to 300 degrees. Heat a large sauté pan or skillet over
medium-high heat. Season the snapper filets with salt on all sides. Add
the canola oil to the sauté pan and sauté the snapper for 1-2 minutes
on each side, starting with the meat side down. Remove the snapper
from the pan and place onto a baking sheet pan. Spread the cilantro
mayonnaise evenly over the meat side of the fish and coat with the corn
tortillas. Place into a preheated 300-degree oven for 6-10 minutes or
until desired doneness is reached. Reserve hot for assembly

For the Orange-Tomatillo Salsa

10 each Tomatillos, husk and stem removed, small diced
5 each Oranges, segmented and small diced
1 tablespoon Cilantro, finely chopped
3 tablespoons Lime juice
Salt to taste

Place the tomatillos and oranges into a bowl and mix with the cilantro
and lime juice. Season with salt to taste and reserve for assembly.

For the Cilantro Mayonnaise

1 cup Mayonnaise
1 teaspoon Cilantro, finely chopped
2 teaspoons Lime juice
Salt to taste

Mix all ingredients in a mixing bowl and season with salt to taste.

BLUEBERRY BUCKLE, MEYER LEMON SORBET AND CHILLED ALMOND SOUP

Serves 8 | *Texas Feast*

For the Assembly

Ladle about 1/4 cup of chilled almond soup into 6 chilled soup bowls. Heat the blueberry buckle in a preheated oven until warmed through. Place in the center of each bowl and place one small scoop of Meyer lemon sorbet on top of the blueberry buckle. Garnish with toasted almonds and fresh blueberries.

THE RECIPE

8 each Blueberry buckles
2 cups Meyer lemon sorbet
3 cups Chilled almond soup

For the Blueberry Buckle

¼ cup Unsalted butter (softened)
¾ cup Sugar
1 each Egg
½ cup Milk
2 ½ cups All purpose flour
1½ teaspoons Baking powder
½ teaspoons Salt
¼ teaspoons Nutmeg
2 cups fresh Blueberries

Preheat oven to 350 degrees. In a mixer using the paddle attachment, cream butter and sugar until light and fluffy. Add egg and mix. Add milk and mix slowly to combine. Add baking powder, salt, nutmeg and flour and mix to combine. Fold in fresh blueberries by hand. Lightly spray a square 10-inch pan with non-stick pan spray and pour in batter. Be sure to smooth batter evenly. Top with streusel topping and bake in a preheated 350-degree oven for about 25 minutes, or until buckle springs back when lightly touched and toothpick comes out clean when inserted. Let cool completely and remove the buckle from the baking dish. Trim edges and cut into 8 equal square portions.

For the Streusel Topping

½ cup sugar
⅓ cup All purpose flour
¼ cup Butter
½ teaspoon Cinnamon

Combine all ingredients in small mixing bowl with the paddle attachment. Mix on speed 3 until ingredients combine and then break apart into small pieces. Sprinkle on top of Blueberry Buckle batter before baking.

For the Meyer Lemon Sorbet

1 cup Meyer lemon juice
1¼ cups Simple syrup
¼ cup Water

Combine all the ingredients in a plastic container and mix well. Mix the night before with a hand blender and let chill in the refrigerator. Turn in an ice cream machine until firm but soft. Sorbet will continue to set in the freezer. Freeze sorbet for 2 hours before using.

For the Simple Syrup

¾ cup Sugar
¾ cup Water

Place all the ingredients into a pot and place on the stove on medium heat. Stir slightly. Bring mixture to a boil until the sugar dissolves. Take off heat and cool completely in the refrigerator before adding to sorbet recipe.

For the Chilled Almond Soup

1½ cups Heavy cream
¼ cup Almond slivers (toasted)
3 tablespoons Frangelico liquor
½ cup Sugar
2 tablespoons Almond paste

Place all of the ingredients into a blender and puree until smooth. Strain though a fine mesh sieve. Refrigerate for about 2 –3 hours or until completely chilled.

CRYSTAL ROOM

Ⓓ

The Crystal Room

During the hotel's restoration, a Cuban cigar box dating back to 1887, horseshoes, and tack were found in the rafters of the horse stables. The stables, on the building's north side (downwind from the patrons), would become The Crystal Room.

VICTORIAN TEA
The Driskill Lobby

THE MENU

Blue Cheese and Red Onion Croustade

Goat Cheese and Chive Crepes with Preserved Lemon

Deviled Crab Finger Sandwich with Cucumber and Dill

Mini Monte Cristo with Smoked Ham and Gruyere Cheese

Rosemary Muffins with Roast Beef and Horseradish Cream

....

Currant Scones ~ Chocolate Dipped Strawberries

Lemon Tartlettes ~ Chocolate Devil's Food Cake

Dried Cherry-Coconut Macaroons ~ Brown Sugar Madeleines

Devonshire Cream ~ Raspberry Jam

For ALMOST THIRTEEN DECADES, The Driskill Lobby has hosted a constant parade of visitors. In the early years, their business may have been with the hotel's Turkish baths, beauty parlor, barber shop or the American National Bank, which opened in 1890 on the hotel's main floor. In recent years, the lobby has become a perfect place to meet for business or pleasure, as well as a place of respite from the hustle and bustle of everyday life.

The Driskill's Victorian Tea will carry you back to a time when all of life moved at a more refined pace. Requiring only a few ingredients and simple preparation, these accompaniments for tea are neither heavy nor filling, just a selection of bite-sized delights to share with family and friends.

THE RECIPE

12 each Croustades
4 ounces Bleu cheese, crumbled
¾ cup Caramelized red onions

For the Croustades

4 slices White bread, crust removed, rolled thin
3 tablespoons Butter melted

Brush the bread with the melted butter and cut into small circles using a fluted cutter. Place the bread circles onto a concave mold and bake for 4-8 minutes or until they are golden brown and crisp.

For the Caramelized Red Onions

1 each Small red onion
1 teaspoon Canola oil
1 teaspoon Butter
1 tablespoon Red wine vinegar
1 tablespoon Sugar

In a large sauté pan add the red onions, canola oil and the butter over medium heat. Cook the onions until they become golden brown and very soft. Add the red wine vinegar and sugar and cook for another 10 minutes over low heat or until all the liquid is evaporated.

BLEU CHEESE AND RED ONION CROUSTADE

Serves 8-12 | *Victorian Tea*

For the Assembly

Preheat oven to 300 degrees. Place the caramelized red onions in the center of the croustade and top with bleu cheese. Place into a preheated 300-degree oven for 3-5 minutes or until the cheese is melted. Serve warm.

GOAT CHEESE AND CHIVE CREPES WITH PRESERVED LEMON

Serves 8-12 | *Victorian Tea*

For the Assembly

Place the crepes on a clean work surface. Using an offset spatula, spread a thick layer of the goat cheese evenly over ¾ of the crepe. Tightly roll the crepe. Trim off excess on each side and bias cut the crepe into 2-3 pieces. Garnish with a slice of preserved lemon and chives.

THE RECIPE

6 ounces Goat cheese (softened)
2 tablespoons Chives, cut into 1/2-inch pieces
6 each Crepes
2 tablespoons Preserved lemon

For the Crepes

½ cup All purpose flour
1 each Egg, beaten
⅔ cup Milk
2 tablespoons Butter, melted
¼ teaspoon Salt

Place all ingredients into a blender and puree until smooth. This batter will keep for up to two days and should rest at least 3 hours. Spray a nonstick 6-inch frying pan with nonstick spray. Over medium heat, fry a small ladle of the batter. Cover only the very bottom of the pan and remove excess batter. Fry the crepe for one minute and turn over for another minute or until golden brown. Reserve at room temperature for assembly.

For the Preserved Lemon

1 teaspoon Salt
2 teaspoons Sugar
1 cup Lemon juice
4 each Lemons, thinly sliced

Place the salt, sugar and lemon juice in a saucepot over medium heat and bring to a boil. Remove from heat and add the sliced lemons. Cool completely and reserve for assembly.

DEVILED CRAB FINGER SANDWICHES WITH CUCUMBER AND DILL

Serves 8-12 | *Victorian Tea*

For the Assembly

Lay out the white bread slices and spread the deviled crab mix evenly over the bread. Top with another slice of bread and cut into even rectangles. Top with a small dollop of the cucumber-dill relish and serve.

THE RECIPE

1 cup Deviled crab mix
6 slices White bread, crust removed
2 tablespoons Cucumber-dill relish

For the Deviled Crab Mix

1 cup Jumbo lump crab meat, shells removed
3 each Eggs, hard boiled, finely grated
1 teaspoon Dijon mustard
1 teaspoon Parsley, finely chopped
1 tablespoon Mayonnaise
½ teaspoon Tabasco
1 teaspoon Lemon juice
Salt to taste

In a mixing bowl, thoroughly mix all of the ingredients except for the crab meat. Fold in the crab meat being careful to maintain the lumps. Season with salt to taste and reserve cold.

For the Cucumber Dill Relish

¼ cup Cucumber, skin and seeds removed, small diced
1 teaspoon Dill, finely chopped
1 teaspoon Lemon juice
Salt to taste

Mix all ingredients together, season with salt to taste and allow to marinate for 10-15 minutes.

MINI MONTE CRISTO WITH SMOKED HAM AND GRUYERE CHEESE

Serves 8-12 | *Victorian Tea*

For the Assembly

Lay the bread slices on a clean work surface and spread the Dijon mustard evenly over the slices. Make one layer of the gruyere cheese. Place the sliced ham on top of the cheese and top with a second layer of gruyere cheese and another slice of white bread. Press the sandwich firmly together, cut the sandwich into four triangles and dip the sandwich into the egg batter. Fry in butter on a preheated griddle or nonstick pan in butter for 2-4 minutes on each side until they are golden brown and hot through the center. Serve immediately.

THE RECIPE

6 each White bread slices
4 ounces Smoked ham, thinly sliced
4 ounces Gruyere cheese, thinly sliced
2-4 tablespoons Dijon mustard
1 cup Egg batter
2 tablespoons Butter

For the Egg Batter

4 each Eggs, beaten
¼ cup Milk
Salt to taste
Pepper to taste

Thoroughly mix ingredients together and reserve cold.

ROSEMARY MUFFINS WITH ROAST BEEF AND HORSERADISH CREAM

Serves 8-12 | *Victorian Tea*

For the Assembly

Cut the rosemary muffin in half and place the sliced roast beef in the center. Top with the horseradish cream and serve.

THE RECIPE

12 each Rosemary muffins
6 ounces Roast beef, thinly sliced
½ cup Horseradish cream

For the Rosemary Muffins

¾ cup All purpose flour
½ teaspoon Baking powder
¼ teaspoon Salt
3 tablespoons Sugar
1 teaspoons Rosemary, finely chopped
1 each Egg, beaten
¼ cup Milk
2 tablespoon Butter, melted

Preheat oven to 375 degrees. Sift flour, baking powder and salt into a bowl. Add the chopped rosemary. Add the egg, milk and melted butter, gently folding together to form a batter. Spoon into 10-12 mini buttered muffin molds and bake in a preheated 375-degree oven for 10-15 minutes or until golden brown.

For the Horseradish Cream

½ cup Sour cream
1 tablespoon Horseradish
1 teaspoon Lemon juice
Salt to taste

Thoroughly mix all ingredients together and season with salt to taste.

BROWN SUGAR MADELEINES

Serves 8-12 | *Victorian Tea*

THE RECIPE

1 cup Unsalted butter
6 each Eggs
¾ cups Sugar
1 pinch Salt
2¼ teaspoons Brown sugar
1 tablespoon Honey
¾ teaspoon Baking powder
1 cup All purpose flour
¼ cup Powdered sugar

Preheat oven to 350 degrees. Grease and lightly flour small Madeleine molds and set aside. Cube butter, and place in a pot on the stove on low heat. Melt butter until it begins to brown, and reserve. In a mixing bowl with the paddle attachment, beat the eggs and the sugar, brown sugar, honey, and salt together. Sift the flour and baking powder together and add to the sugar-egg mixture and mix until well combined. Set mixer on low speed and pour in the browned butter slowly. Mix well. Fill prepared Madeleine molds half way and bake in a preheated 350-degree oven for 8-10 minutes. Dust lightly with powdered sugar and serve.

CURRANT SCONES

Serves 8-12 | *Victorian Tea*

THE RECIPE

1 cup Butter, unsalted, cubed and cold
⅓ cup Sugar
1¾ cups Cake flour
1¾ cups Bread flour
1½ tablespoons Baking powder
¼ teaspoon Salt
3 each Eggs
1½ cups Milk
1½ cups Currants
2 each Eggs (for the egg wash)
6 tablespoons Water (for the egg wash)
All purpose flour or bread flour (for rolling out)

Preheat oven to 350 degrees. Sift the sugar, cake flour, bread flour, baking powder and salt together in a kitchen aid mixing bowl. Using a paddle attachment, incorporate the cold butter cubes. Stop the mixer when the butter is in pea size chunks. With the mixer on low speed, slowly add the eggs and milk. Add the currants and mix until it forms a dough. Place dough on a well-floured surface, and roll out to about ¼ inch thickness. Use plenty of all purpose or bread flour to roll out. Cut into desired shape and size. Dust off excess flour using a dry pastry brush. Place on a parchment-lined baking sheet. Mix the eggs with the water to form an egg wash and brush the tops of the scones. Bake in a preheated 350-degree oven for about 15 minutes or until golden brown.

RASPBERRY JAM

Serves 8-12 | *Victorian Tea*

THE RECIPE

2 pints Raspberries
½ cup Sugar

Place all ingredients into a saucepot and bring to a boil. Place mixture into a blender and puree until smooth. Cool completely and serve in small ramekins.

LEMON TARTLETTES

Serves 8-12 | *Victorian Tea*

For the Assembly

Using a pastry bag with plain tip, pipe the lemon curd into pre-baked tart shells. Place in a preheated 350-degree oven for 3-5 minutes or until curd sets. Allow to cool and serve.

DRIED CHERRY-COCONUT MACAROONS

Serves 8-12 | *Victorian Tea*

THE RECIPE

1 pint Lemon curd
1 recipe Tart dough

For the Tart Dough

1 cup + 1 tablespoons Powdered sugar
½ cup unsalted Butter (softened)
1¼ cups All purpose flour
1 each Eggs

Preheat oven to 350 degrees. Lightly spray mini muffin pan with pan spray and set aside. Cream the powdered sugar and the butter together in a mixing bowl. Add the flour and mix until incorporated. Add the eggs and mix until well combined and mixture forms a dough. Remove dough from bowl and wrap with plastic wrap. Refrigerate for 1 hour or until chilled. On a well-floured surface, roll out the dough until it reaches ⅛ of an inch thick. Using a round cutter, cut out circles and press into mini muffin pans. Trim off excess. Place in freezer until frozen. Place in preheated 350 degree oven and bake for about 10-12 minutes. Remove from oven and allow to cool.

For the Lemon Curd

3 each Eggs
3 each Yolks
1 cup Sugar
½ cup Fresh lemon juice
⅓ cup Unsalted butter, softened

Place eggs, egg yolks, sugar and lemon juice into a bowl and combine using a wire whisk. Set bowl over a double broiler over low heat. Stir and cook the mixture until it thickens enough to hold a line when youy drag your finger over the surface. Add the butter off of heat and incorporate. Strain the mixture through a sieve. Allow curd to cool completely and chill over the surface. Refrigerate 2-3 hours for best use.

THE RECIPE

1½ cups Sugar
1⅓ cups Flake coconut
⅓ cup Bread flour
¾ cup Egg whites
1 cup Sugar
1 teaspoon Vanilla extract
½ cup Dried cherries

Preheat oven to 350 degrees. Combine the 1½ cups sugar, coconut, and bread flour in a separate bowl; set aside. Place the egg whites, sugar and vanilla into a bowl and whip until stiff peaks form and the mixture triples in volume. Add the sugar, flake coconut, and bread flour into whipped egg whites. Gently fold the mixture together until well combined. Using a small scoop or spoon, drop the macaroons onto a parchment-lined baking sheet. Press a dried cherry into the center of each ball. Bake in a preheated 350-degree oven for 4-6 minutes. Rotate and bake for 4-6 minutes more or until lightly golden brown.

CHOCOLATE DIPPED STRAWBERRIES

Serves 8-12 | *Victorian Tea*

CHOCOLATE DEVIL'S FOOD CAKE

Serves 8-12 | *Victorian Tea*

For the Assembly

Place onto a baking sheet and pour on warmed chocolate glaze. Smooth out the glaze and cover the top of the cake. Refrigerate until the glaze is set. Cut the glazed devils food cake into small rectangles or squares and serve.

THE RECIPE

24 each Fresh strawberries
1 lb. Dark chocolate coating
1 lb. White chocolate coating

Chop half of the dark and white chocolate. Place separately in bowls over a double boiler on low heat. Stir occasionally. Prepare strawberries by wiping them off with a damp cloth. Do not run under water. With the remaining chocolate, using a vegetable peeler, shave chocolate into separated piles and reserve. When the chocolate is melted, dip the strawberries in one at a time holding on at the hull. Scrape off the excess on the side of the bowl, and dip into the opposite color of chocolate shavings. Set to dry on a parchment-lined baking sheet.

THE RECIPE

1 baking sheet Devil's food cake
2 cups Chocolate glaze

For the Devil's Food Cake

2 cups Hot water
½ cup Cocoa powder
2⅓ cups All purpose flour
3¾ cups Sugar
1½ teaspoons Salt
2½ teaspoons Baking soda
2 cups Buttermilk
1½ cups Vegetable oil
3 each Eggs

Preheat oven to 350 degrees. Grease a baking sheet with pan spray and line with parchment paper. In a mixing bowl, whisk together the cocoa powder and hot water slowly until well incorporated and there are no lumps. Sift all purpose flour, sugar, salt, and baking soda into a separate mixing bowl. In a separate container, combine the buttermilk, oil, and eggs. In a mixer, add the dry ingredients and slowly add half the buttermilk mixture. Scrape down the sides of bowl, and then add the remaining buttermilk mixture. Mix until combined. On low speed, add half of the cocoa powder water mixture and scrape down the sides. Add the remaining cocoa powder water mixture and mix until incorporated. Let cake batter rest for 15-20 minutes before baking. Pour batter into prepared pan and fill half-way up the sides of the pan. Bake in a preheated 350-degree oven for 25-30 minutes or until cake springs back when touched and toothpick comes out clean when inserted. Cool completely and unmold onto the back of another baking sheet and refrigerate.

For the Chocolate Glaze

1½ cups Quality semi-sweet chocolate
8 ounces Unsalted butter
2 teaspoons Vanilla extract
1 tablespoon Corn syrup

Place all of the ingredients in a large bowl and set over a double boiler on low heat. With a rubber spatula, stir mixture occasionally until melted and incorporated. Reserve warm for assembly.

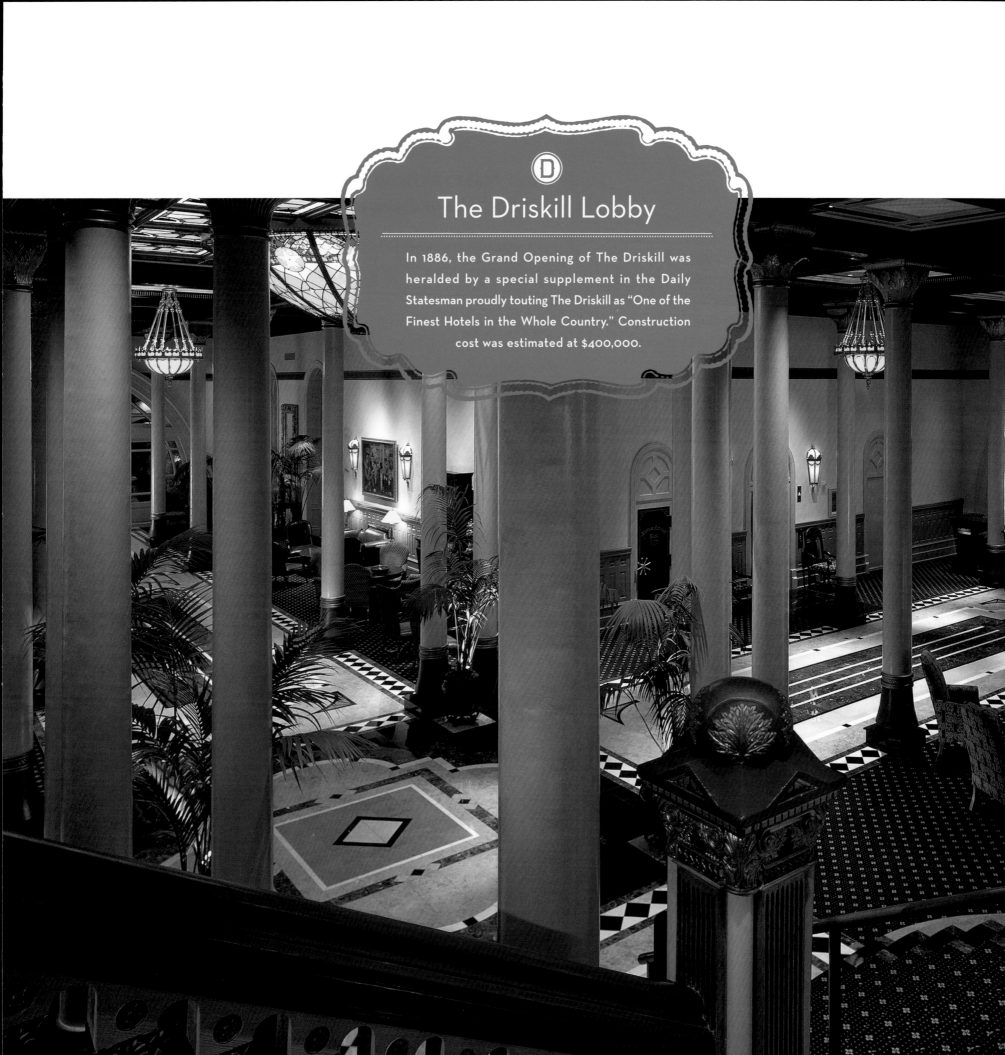

The Driskill Lobby

In 1886, the Grand Opening of The Driskill was heralded by a special supplement in the Daily Statesman proudly touting The Driskill as "One of the Finest Hotels in the Whole Country." Construction cost was estimated at $400,000.

ROMANTIC DINNER FOR TWO
The Driskill Grill

THE MENU

Cream of Porcini Mushroom Soup with Baked Brie

Baby Spinach Salad with Fried Oysters

Pan Broiled Lobster with Celery Root Puree, Watercress, and Black Truffle Butter

Red Velvet Cake with Champagne Sabayon, and Candied Pecans

With The Driskill Grill receiving accolades from food writers across the country and patrons from around the world, what could be better than to sample some of the Grill's delights in your own home?

Just as with the ever-changing selection of exciting new dishes at the grill, these recipes offer a chance to elicit oohs and aahs from that special someone on Valentine's Day or an anniversary. As at the Grill, we recommend matching wines (try small bottles or "splits") with individual courses. And don't forget the candles.

CREAM OF PORCINI MUSHROOM SOUP

For the Assembly

Place the baked brie into the center of two large soup bowls. Make a small cut into the top of the brie and place the fried porcinis into the cut. Garnish with micro cabbage or similar micro green or parsley. Slowly pour the hot mushroom soup into the bowl at the table and serve.

THE RECIPE

2 cups Cream of wild mushroom soup
2 each Baked brie
6 each Fried porcini mushrooms
Micro cabbage for garnish, may substitute Italian flat leaf parsley

For the Cream of Porcini Mushroom Soup

2 tablespoons Canola oil
3 tablespoons Whole butter
1 cup (½ pound) Fresh porcini mushrooms, cleaned and chopped
3 each Shallots, finely chopped
2 each Garlic cloves, finely chopped
1 tablespoon Brandy
1 teaspoon Sherry
2 cups Chicken stock
½ cup Heavy whipping cream
Sherry wine to taste
Lemon juice to taste
Salt to taste

In a large saucepot add the canola oil and butter over medium heat. Allow the butter and oil to get hot and sauté the porcini mushrooms for 3-5 minutes or until golden brown. Add the shallots and garlic and allow them to sweat for 2-3 minutes. Add the brandy and the sherry and reduce by half. Add the chicken stock and bring to a boil. Cook at a low simmer for 15 minutes over low heat. Remove ⅓ of the soup and puree in a blender until smooth. Add the puree back into the soup and bring back to a simmer. Add the heavy whipping cream and season with sherry, lemon juice and salt to taste. Reserve hot for assembly.

For the Baked Brie

1 each Miniature brie wheel
6 ounces Puff pastry
1 each Egg, whipped
1 tablespoon Water

Preheat oven to 300 degrees. Cut the brie cheese into two equal circles using a round cutter. Roll out the puff pastry to ⅛-inch thick by 3-inch circles. Mix the whipped egg and water together to form an egg wash. Place the brie pieces into the puff pastry and brush all edges with egg wash. Fold and tuck the puff pastry around the brie creating a seal with the egg wash. Pinch all sides. Turn over and brush all sides with egg wash. Place into a preheated 300-degree oven for 8-10 minutes or until the brie is warmed through and the puff pastry is crisp. Reserve hot for assembly.

For the Fried Porcini Mushrooms

2 each Porcini mushrooms, thinly sliced
¼ cup All purpose flour
1 each Egg, whipped
Salt to taste

Preheat frying oil to 350 degrees. Dredge the sliced porcini mushrooms in the all purpose flour and then dip into the whipped egg. Dredge again in the all purpose flour and then fry in preheated oil for 2-3 minutes or until golden brown and crisp. Season with salt to taste.

BABY SPINACH SALAD WITH FRIED OYSTERS

Serves 2 | *Romantic Dinner for Two*

For the Assembly

On two elongated salad plates, place three individual piles of the spinach salad equal distances apart. Place one fried oyster on top of each pile. Using a spoon, drizzle the remaining vinaigrette across the front of each plate and serve.

THE RECIPE

2 cups Baby spinach salad
½ cup Mustard vinaigrette
6 each Fried oysters

For the Baby Spinach Salad

1½ cups Baby spinach, fine julienne
½ cup Mache or watercress leaves
1 each Red bell pepper, roasted, peeled and julienne
2 tablespoons Mustard vinaigrette
Salt to taste

In a mixing bowl combine the spinach, mache and roasted red bell peppers. Toss gently with only 2 tablespoons of the mustard vinaigrette, reserving the remaining vinaigrette for assembly. Season with salt to taste.

For the Mustard Vinaigrette

½ cup Whole grain mustard
1 each Lemon, juiced
1 teaspoon Honey
1 tablespoon Olive oil
Salt to taste

In a mixing bowl using a wire whip, incorporate the mustard, lemon juice, honey and olive oil. Season with salt to taste.

For the Fried Oysters

¼ cup All purpose flour
¼ cup Semolina flour
6 each Gulf oysters, shucked
Salt to taste

Preheat frying oil to 350 degrees. Mix together the all purpose flour and semolina flour. Thoroughly coat each oyster with the flour mixture and fry in preheated 350 degree oil for 2-3 minutes or until golden brown. Season with salt to taste and reserve hot for assembly.

PAN BROILED LOBSTER WITH CELERY ROOT PUREE, WATERCRESS, AND BLACK TRUFFLE BUTTER

Serves 2 | *Romantic Dinner for Two*

For the Assembly

Spread the celery root puree on the bottom of two large dinner plates. Intertwine the lobster tails together and place them in the center of the celery root puree. Garnish with watercress and ladle or spoon the black truffle butter on the side of the plate.

THE RECIPE

2 each Broiled lobster tails
1 cup Celery root puree
½ cup Black truffle butter
¼ cup Watercress, sprigs

For the Broiled Lobster Tail

1 tablespoon Canola oil
2 tablespoons Butter
2 each 8-ounce lobster tails, split in half lengthwise
Salt to taste

Preheat oven to 400 degrees. In a large oven-proof sauté pan add the canola oil and butter over high heat. Season the lobsters with salt to taste and sauté the split lobster tails, meat side down for 3 minutes or until the meat is golden brown. Place into preheated oven and cook for 5-6 minutes or until the meat is easily removable from the shell. Remove the lobsters from the oven and allow them to cool slightly. Using a fork or kitchen tongs gently pry the meat from the shell only removing 90 percent of the meat and keeping the tail-end intact. Intertwine two tails together and place back into the oven to get hot just before assembly.

For the Celery Root Puree

1 each Celery root, 3-4 inches in diameter, peeled and large diced
Water as needed
Salt to taste
2 tablespoons Butter
½ cup Heavy cream
Salt to taste

Preheat oven to 300 degrees. In a large pot add the diced celery root and cover with water. Season the water with a generous amount of salt. Bring to a boil over high heat. Turn down to a simmer and cook until the celery root is cooked through and is fork tender. Combine the butter and heavy cream in a sauce pot and bring to a boil. Reserve hot for the celery root. Gently strain the celery root and place into preheated oven to dry for 3-5 minutes. Add the celery root and hot cream and butter mixture to a blender or mixer and puree the celery root until smooth. Season with salt to taste and reserve hot until assembly.

For the Black Truffle Butter

1 tablespoon Canola oil
2 each Shallots, roughly chopped
1 teaspoon Fennel seed
1 teaspoon Whole black peppercorns
1 each Bay leaf
1 cup White wine
1½ cups Heavy whipping cream
6 ounces Whole butter, cut into ½-inch pieces, room temperature
1 each Black truffle, medium size, finely diced
1 teaspoon White truffle oil
1 each Lemon, juiced
Salt to taste

In a medium-sized sauce pot over medium heat add the canola oil. Add the shallots, fennel seed, black peppercorns, and bay leaf and sauté for 2-3 minutes, being careful not to gain any color on the shallots. Add the white wine and reduce by 90 percent. Add the heavy cream and reduce 90 percent. Take the pot off of the heat and add the butter piece by piece while whisking continuously. Strain through a fine mesh sieve and reserve warm. In a small sauté pan, sauté the black truffles with the truffle oil for 1 minute or until fragrant. Add the sautéed black truffles to the butter sauce and season with lemon juice, and salt to taste.

RED VELVET CAKE WITH CHAMPAGNE SABAYON AND CANDIED PECANS

Serves 2 | *Romantic Dinner for Two*

For the Assembly

Spoon equal portions of the champagne sabayon onto the center of two large plates. Cut out one triangular wedge from each dome and place the dome on top of the sabayon. Place two of the candied pecans in the cut-out wedge. Place the tuille on top of the dome and encircle with the pecans. Dollop 2-3 cherries with sauce around the plate and serve.

Pre-Assembly

In dome flexi-molds, pipe in white chocolate mousse and smooth out. Place a red velvet cake circle layer on top of the white chocolate mousse and press lightly ensuring that there are no air pockets. Freeze overnight, then unmold, and place back in freezer on a glazing rack with a parchment-paper-lined baking sheet. Ladle on red-white chocolate glaze completely covering the domes and place the domes into refrigerator until ready to serve.

For the White Chocolate Mousse

1½ ounces White chocolate (chopped)
1 each Egg white
1 tablespoon Sugar
¼ cup Heavy cream
1 teaspoon Gelatin
1 tablespoon Grande Marnier

Place the white chocolate over a double boiler and melt. Place the egg whites and the sugar over a separate double boiler and whisk until sugar dissolves. Whip the egg whites in a mixer until the egg whites reach stiff peaks. Whip the heavy cream to soft peaks and set aside in a cool place. In a small sauce pot, warm the Grand Marnier and add gelatin. Dissolve the gelatin in the Grande Marnier and add to the melted white chocolate. Remove the white chocolate from the double boiler and gently fold in the egg whites and then the whipped cream. Using a piping bag, pipe the white chocolate mousse into the dome flexi-molds.

THE RECIPE

2 each Red velvet domes
2 each Sumac tuiles
4 each Candied pecans
½ cup Champagne sabayon
¼ cup Cherry reduction

For the Red Velvet Cakes

¾ cup Red-white Chocolate Glaze
1 recipe Red velvet cake
1 recipe White chocolate mousse

For the Red Velvet Cake

½ cup Shortening
2 tablespoons Unsalted butter (softened)
1½ cups Sugar
3 each Eggs
1 teaspoon Vanilla extract
1 tablespoon Red food coloring
1½ tablespoons Cocoa powder
1 teaspoon Salt
2 cups Cake flour
1⅓ cup Buttermilk
1 teaspoon Baking soda
1½ teaspoons Vinegar

Preheat the oven to 350 degrees and pan spray and parchment line a baking sheet. Cream the shortening, butter and sugar in a mixer until light and fluffy. Combine the eggs, vanilla extract, red food coloring, and buttermilk using a wire whisk. Slowly add the egg mixture to the butter-sugar mixture. Scrape down the sides of the bowl. Sift the cocoa powder, salt, and cake flour together and add to the mixture in two parts. Scrape down sides in between the additions of the flour mixture. Combine the vinegar and baking soda together in a separate bowl and add to the mixture until well combined. Pour into prepared pan and bake for about 25-30 minutes or until cake springs back when touched and toothpick comes out clean when inserted. Let cool completely, then unmold. When cool, using a round cutter, cut out circles the same size as the open part of the dome molds.

For the Sumac Tuiles

2 ounces Unsalted butter
⅓ cup Sugar
¼ cup All purpose flour
⅓ cup Egg whites, room temperature
½ ounce Sumac powder

Preheat oven to 350 degrees. Using a mixer with the paddle attachment, cream the butter and sugar. Slowly add the egg whites. Add the flour and mix until incorporated. Using a silt pad on the back of a baking sheet, lay down a rectangular stencil. With an off-set spatula, smooth down the sumac tuile paste until it is an even thickness. Remove stencil and repeat until the necessary quantity is prepared. Lightly sprinkle sumac powder on top of the paste and bake in a preheated 350-degree oven for 2-5 minutes or until lightly brown. Using an off-set spatula, peel off the cookies and wrap quickly, while still hot, around a French rolling pin. Remove as soon as cool and repeat with the remaining tuiles. Reserve tuiles in a cool dry place until assembly.

For the Cherry Reduction

¾ cup Sugar
¾ cup Water
¾ cup Sour cherry puree
½ cup Port wine
2 ounces Cherries (in syrup)

Combine all the ingredients, except the cherries, in a pot and place over medium heat and bring to a boil. Reduce by half and strain through a fine mesh sieve. Fold in the cherries and reserve warm for assembly.

For the Red-White Chocolate Glaze

4 ounces White chocolate (chopped)
⅛ cup Heavy cream
1 teaspoon Red food coloring

Melt the white chocolate over a double boiler, and set aside. Boil the heavy cream with the red food coloring and add to the chocolate and mix until well combined.

For the Caramelized Pecans

1 cup Sugar
2 teaspoons Water
4-6 each Pecan halves

Place the sugar and the water in a pot and mix. Wash down the sides of the pot with a pastry brush dipped in water and place on the stove over medium-low heat. Cook and caramelize the sugar for 5-10 minutes or until it becomes a light amber color. Carefully skewer each pecan with wooden skewers. Place a pan or dish on the floor next to a table. Dip the pecans in the caramelized sugar and place the skewer down on a table with the pecan hanging off the edge, allowing the excess sugar to drip down into the pan or dish and to form long strips of sugar. When cool, remove the skewer and lay the pecans flat in a cool dry place until assembly.

For the Champagne Sabayon

2 each Egg yolks
2 tablespoons Sugar
¼ cup Champagne

Combine the yolks, sugar and champagne in a bowl— then whip together until they are thoroughly blended. Place the bowl over a double boiler and beat the mixture with a wire whisk until it becomes thick and foamy. Serve immediately.

Ⓓ The Driskill Grill

The portraits in The Grill are of James "Pa" Ferguson and his wife "Ma." After Pa's impeachment from governor in 1917, Ma won the ensuing November general election and became the second woman governor in U.S. history.

WINE AND CHEESE RECEPTION
The Maximillian Room

THE MENU

Baked Baby Pears with Boursin Cheese and Honey Spiced Walnuts

Blueberry Conserve with Maytag Crackers

Monterey Jack Cheese Fondue with Jalapeno Cornbread

Prosciutto-Wrapped Cantaloupe and Port Salute with Vanilla-Muscato Gastrique

Warm Camembert with Roasted Garlic and Sourdough Bread

Goat Cheese, Smoked Bacon, and Hearts of Romaine with Fried Leeks

above - The Maximillian Room served as the Men's Smoking Room for many years. Across the Mezzanine Level, the ladies retired to the Ladies Parlor, located in the Jim Hogg Room, shown here.

JUST OFF THE DRISKILL MEZZANINE, the Maximillian Room was originally the men's smoking room. In the 1930s, an antique shop in San Antonio discovered eight massive gold leaf mirrors that were meant to be a gift from the Mexican Emperor Maximillian to his wife, the Empress Carlotta, both of whom had been placed on the throne by Napoleon III. With nationalism in Mexico running high, the Mexican people rejected foreign rule and rebelled. The French troops withdrew from Mexico City, leaving behind the idealistic Maximillian who refused to abdicate in the belief that he could regain support and lead Mexico to greatness. Maximillian was executed on June 10, 1867 and Carlotta—rumored to be mad with grief—relocated to Belgium and Italy, living in seclusion for the last sixty years of her life.

Carlotta never saw the beautiful mirrors ordered by her husband. Made in France with a reflective backing of sterling silver and crushed diamonds, the mirrors still show a remarkable sparkle in their reflections. Three years after Carlotta's death, The Driskill purchased the mirrors and converted the men's smoking room to a dining room that would remain the ultimate Austin dining spot for the next forty years.

Today the Maximillian Room is frequently used for special catering events, particularly during the many charity fund-raisers held on the Mezzanine level. The Maximillian Room recently served as the meeting place for Texas-born actor Fess Parker—who became a national icon playing Davy Crockett in the fifties—and Oscar-winner Billy Bob Thornton—who was then playing Colonel Crockett in the Disney feature film, "The Alamo."

The accompanying recipes—emphasizing cheese and its natural pairing with wines and other ingredients that help to contrast the cheese—are perfect for a stand-up dinner party at home. Most important, these sophisticated ingredients and taste and texture combinations will wow your guests without you spending all day in the kitchen.

BAKED BABY PEARS AND BOURSIN CHEESE
WITH HONEY SPICED WALNUTS

Serves 12 | *Wine and Cheese Reception*

For the Assembly

Preheat oven to 300 degrees. Bake the pears
until golden brown and warmed through being
careful not to burn the walnuts. Arrange the
pears onto a platter and serve.

THE RECIPE

12 each Baked baby pears, D'Anjou or similar
4 cups Spiced walnuts

For the Baby Baked Pears

12 each Baby pears
4 ounces Butter
1 tablespoon Brown sugar
2 cups Boursin cheese, softened
4 cups Spiced walnuts
1 cup Honey

Preheat oven to 300 degrees. Peel the pears on all sides being careful to
keep the stem attached. Cut off the very bottom portion of the pear until
it sits flat. Using a melon baller and starting at the bottom, remove the
core and all of the seeds, hollowing out the center of the pear. Place pears
onto a baking sheet. Add the butter and brown sugar to a saucepot and
bring to a boil. Brush the pears thoroughly with the brown sugar-butter
mixture and place in a preheated 300-degree oven and cook for 5-7
minutes or until pears are tender but still have a crunch. Allow the pears
to cool completely and stuff with the boursin cheese. Roll the pears gently
in honey, coating all sides, top and bottom. Gently coat and pack the pears
with the spiced walnuts on all sides. Place the stuffed and crusted pears
into the refrigerator and reserve cold for assembly.

For the Spiced Walnuts

4 cups Walnuts, lightly toasted
1 tablespoon Powdered sugar
2 tablespoons Cayenne
1 teaspoon Salt

Place all ingredients into a food processor and pulse until ground fine.

BLUEBERRY CONSERVE WITH MAYTAG CRACKERS

Serves 12 | *Wine and Cheese Reception*

For the Assembly

Place a small dollop of the blueberry conserve on each of the maytag crackers and garnish with a small sprig of mint and powdered sugar.

THE RECIPE

12 each Maytag crackers
¾ cup Blueberry conserve
½ cup Crumbled Maytag bleu cheese
Small mint sprigs for garnish
Powdered sugar for garnish

For the Maytag Crackers

6 ounces Maytag bleu cheese
1 tablespoon All purpose flour

Preheat oven to 300 degrees. Using a mixer with a paddle attachment, mix the maytag bleu cheese and the flour together until completely incorporated. Mold the cheese into 1½-inch logs using plastic wrap and place into the freezer for 1 hour. Using a knife dipped into warm water, slice thin discs of the cheese mixture and place each disc onto a Silpat(nonstick baking sheet). Place into a preheated 300-degree oven for 7-9 minutes or until golden brown. Using a plastic pipe or stainless steel mold, place the cheese discs, while still hot, over the pipe to form a concave shape. If the cheese cools and cannot be formed, place back into the oven for one minute and repeat process.

For the Blueberry Conserve

1 pint Fresh blueberries
¼ cup Sugar
½ cup Red wine

In a medium-sized saucepot add one half of the blueberries. Add the sugar and the red wine. Cook over low-medium heat for 15-20 minutes or until the mixture becomes thick. Fold in the remainder of the blueberries and stir. Refrigerate until completely cold and reserve for assembly.

MONTEREY JACK CHEESE FONDUE WITH JALAPENO CORNBREAD

Serves 12 | *Wine and Cheese Reception*

For the Assembly

Place the hot fondue into a cast-iron dish, fondue pot, or small ceramic dishes. Dice the corn bread into small cubes and skewer. Place the cornbread skewers around the fondue and serve.

THE RECIPE

2 cups Monterey Jack cheese fondue
½ sheet / 20-25 cubes Jalapeno cornbread

For the Monterey Jack Cheese Fondue

2 tablespoons Butter
2 tablespoons All purpose flour
¼ teaspoon Cumin, ground
1½ cups Heavy whipping cream
2 ounces Dark, Texas beer
12 ounces Monterey Jack cheese
Salt to taste

In a large size saucepot add the butter and allow to boil. Over medium heat, whisk in the flour and cook for 3 minutes. Add the cumin and cook for 1 minute. Whisk in the heavy whipping cream and bring mixture to a boil. Add the beer and return mixture to a boil. Reduce heat to low and whisk in the Monterey Jack cheese. Place mixture into a blender and puree until smooth. Season with salt to taste. Reserve hot for assembly.

For the Jalapeno Cornbread

¾ cup Bread flour
¾ cup All purpose flour
1½ cups Cornmeal
¾ cup Sugar
1 tablespoon Baking powder
Salt to taste
4 ounces Unsalted butter, melted
3 cups Milk
3 each Eggs
½ cup Jalapenos, seeds and stem removed, finely chopped

Preheat oven to 350 degrees. Grease and parchment-line a baking sheet. Place all of the dry ingredients into a mixer with a paddle attachment and mix well. Combine the eggs and milk together in a separate container. While the machine is running on low, slowly add the milk-egg mixture to the dry ingredients and incorporate. Add the melted butter and gently fold in the jalapenos. Pour and smooth into the baking sheet or oven-proof shallow baking pan and bake in a preheated 350-degree oven for 15-20 minutes or until it springs back to the touch and is golden brown.

PROSCIUTTO-WRAPPED CANTALOUPE AND PORT SALUTE WITH VANILLA-MUSCATO GASTRIQUE

Serves 12 | *Wine and Cheese Reception*

For the Assembly

Place the wrapped cantaloupe and port salute onto a serving tray alternating the colors back and forth. Spoon the vanilla-muscato gastrique over the prosciutto-wrapped cantaloupe and port salute and serve.

THE RECIPE

12 each Prosciutto-wrapped cantaloupe and port salute
¾ cup Vanilla-muscato gastrique

For the Vanilla-Muscato Gastrique

½ cup Muscato wine
2 tablespoons Cider vinegar
1 each Vanilla bean, split
1 teaspoon Vanilla extract
2 tablespoon Sugar

Place all ingredients into a small sauce pot and bring to a boil. Strain through a fine mesh sieve and completely cool mixture, Reserve for assembly.

For the Prosciutto-Wrapped Cantaloupe and Port Salute

1 each Small cantaloupe, peeled, seeds removed, cut into 1-inch cubes
8 ounces Port salute cheese, rind removed, cut into 1-inch cubes
8 ounces Prosciutto, thinly sliced and cut into 1-inch by 3-inch rectangles

Lay the prosciutto on a flat service. Place one piece of cantaloupe and one piece of port salute next to each other and tightly wrap the outside with the prosciutto.

WARM CAMEMBERT WITH ROASTED GARLIC AND SOURDOUGH BREAD

Serves 12 | *Wine and Cheese Reception*

For the Assembly

Place the warm camembert onto a platter and place sliced pieces of toasted sourdough bread around the cheese. Place the whole roasted bulbs of garlic around the cheese and serve.

THE RECIPE

1 each Camembert wheel
3 each Roasted garlic bulbs
Sliced sourdough as needed

For the Warm Camembert

1 each Camembert cheese wheel, 8-10 ounces

Preheat oven to 350 degrees. Place the camembert cheese on a greased sheet pan and place into oven. Bake for 5-10 minutes or until the center of the cheese is warmed through.

For the Roasted Garlic Bulbs

Garlic bulbs
Olive oil as needed

Preheat oven to 300 degrees. Rub each bulb with olive oil and bake for 12-16 minutes or until the garlic cloves are soft. Remove from oven and while still hot cut off the top of the bulb exposing the roasted garlic. Serve immediately.

GOAT CHEESE, SMOKED BACON, AND HEARTS OF ROMAINE, WITH FRIED LEEKS

Serves 12 | *Wine and Cheese Reception*

For the Assembly

Place the goat cheese into the center of the romaine heart.

Top with rendered crisp bacon and fried leeks and serve.

THE RECIPE

6 ounce Goat cheese, softened
4 ounces Smoked bacon, cut into small squares, rendered crisp
3 tablespoons Fried leeks
1 each Hearts of romaine, cut into small wedges

For the Fried Leeks

1 each Leek, white part only, cut into fine julienne
Water as needed
Salt to taste

Preheat frying oil to 300 degrees. Bring the water to a boil and blanch the julienne leeks for 1 minute. Place into an ice bath and shock until cold. Strain and remove excess water. Fry in preheated 300-degree oil until slightly brown. Drain and place on paper towels to dry. Season with salt to taste.

The Maximillian Room

Empress Carlotta never saw the mirrors ordered for her by her husband, Emperor Maximillian of Mexico. With a reflective backing of sterling silver and crushed diamonds, the mirrors still show a remarkable sparkle in their reflections.

THANKSGIVING FEAST
The Citadel Club

THE MENU

Oven Roasted Turkey

Sausage-Corn-Bread Stuffing

Jalapeno-Cranberry Relish

Sugar Mashed Turnips

Green Bean Casserole with Fried Onions

Homemade Apple Cider

Pumpkin Crème Brûlée and Linzer Leaf Cookies

LOCATED IN THE 1928 TOWER ADDITION, the Citadel Club was originally occupied by The Driskill Drugstore, then by the private Headliner's Club, and finally—starting in 1966—by the equally exclusive Citadel Club whose all male membership devoted long hours of conversation to politics, the arts and the natural wonders of Texas. The exclusion of women from the club was one of the primary factors in the club's demise.

Now a popular spot for both business conferences and wedding receptions, the free-flowing rooms of the Citadel still have the feel of an exclusive, "old" Texas club. A Thanksgiving feast here would just as easily satisfy the tastes of contemporary Texans as it would the membership of the early Driskill clubs, including the three greats of early Texas literature—Walter Prescott Webb, Roy Bedichek and J. Frank Dobie—who shared many a meal and conversation at their home away from home, The Driskill.

above - Cactus Pryor (l) and Fess Parker at The Headliners Club, c. 1966

OVEN ROASTED TURKEY

Serves 6-8 | *Thanksgiving Feast*

For the Assembly

Place the turkey on a decorative serving platter on top of the sausage cornbread stuffing and serve with the pan gravy.

THE RECIPE

1 each Whole turkey
6 cups Pan gravy

For the Oven Roasted Turkey

1 each Whole turkey, 12-14 lbs.
8 ounces Unsalted butter, softened
Salt and pepper to taste

Rub turkey with unsalted butter and season with salt and pepper. Preheat oven to 500 degrees, roast the turkey until golden brown for about 15-20 minutes. Turn the temperature down to 300 degrees and cook for about 1½ to 2 hours or until the turkey is cooked through and the juices run clear. Strain the pan drippings through a fine mesh sieve and reserve for the gravy and the stuffing.

For the Pan Gravy

1 cup Pan drippings, fat removed
½ cup Onions, chopped
½ cup Celery, chopped
½ cup Carrots, chopped
2 tablespoons Garlic, chopped
8 ounces Giblets, ground
⅓ cup All purpose flour
½ cup Red wine
2 quarts Chicken or turkey stock
2 tablespoons Fresh sage, chopped
Salt to taste

In a large saucepot add the pan drippings over medium heat. Add the onions, celery, carrots and garlic and sauté for 4-6 minutes or until the onions become translucent. Add the giblets and cook for 10 minutes. Add the flour and stir until the flour coats the vegetables. Add the red wine and reduce by half. Add the turkey stock and bring the liquid to a boil. Add the sage and puree the gravy until desired consistency. Season with salt to taste and reserve hot.

SAUSAGE-CORN-BREAD STUFFING

Serves 6-8 | *Thanksgiving Feast*

For the Assembly

Place the sausage-corn-bread stuffing onto a serving platter
and serve with the roasted turkey.

THE RECIPE

8 cups Sausage-Corn-Bread Stuffing

For the Sausage-Corn-Bread Stuffing

½ cup Pan drippings, fat removed
1 pound Italian sausage
2 cups Onion, small diced
1½ cups Celery, small diced
3 tablespoons Garlic, minced
3 tablespoons Shallots, minced
8 cups Chicken or turkey Stock
2 tablespoons Sage, finely chopped
6 cups Corn bread, cubed and toasted
Salt to taste

In a large sauté pan add the pan drippings over medium heat. Add the sausage
and cook until done. Drain the sausage and return back to the pan. Add the
onion, celery, garlic and shallots and sauté for 3-4 minutes. Add the chicken
stock and chopped sage. Bring to a boil and add the diced cornbread. Mix
thoroughly, season with salt to taste and reserve hot for assembly.

JALAPENO-CRANBERRY RELISH

Serves 6-8 | *Thanksgiving Feast*

For the Assembly

Place the jalapeno-cranberry relish into a relish dish and serve.

THE RECIPE

4 cups Jalapeno-cranberry relish

For the Jalapeno-Cranberry Relish

4 cups Cranberries
2 each Large jalapeno peppers, seeds and stems removed
15 leaves Cilantro, stems removed
2 tablespoons Orange zest
½ cup Maple syrup
Salt to taste

Place the cranberries, jalapenos, cilantro and orange zest
into a food processor and pulse until desired consistency.
Add the maple syrup and season with salt to taste.

SUGAR MASHED TURNIPS

Serves 6-8 | *Thanksgiving Feast*

For the Assembly

Place the sugar mashed turnips into a serving dish
and sprinkle brown sugar on top.

THE RECIPE

6 cups Sugar mashed turnips
½ cup Brown sugar

For the Sugar Mashed Turnips

8 each Turnips, peeled and quartered
2 each Medium-size potatoes, peeled and quartered
Water as needed
Salt
4 ounces Butter, softened
4 tablespoons Brown sugar

Preheat oven to 300 degrees. In a large saucepot add the turnips, cover with
water and season heavily with salt. Bring to a boil and simmer for 10-15
minutes or until the turnips are soft. In another saucepot add the potatoes,
cover with water and season heavily with salt. Bring to a boil and simmer
for 10-15 minutes or until the potatoes are soft. Drain both the turnips and
potatoes and place in a preheated 300-degree oven for 5 minutes or until
the turnips and potatoes are dry. Rice the turnips and potatoes together and
add the softened butter, brown sugar, and season with salt to taste.

GREEN BEAN CASSEROLE WITH FRIED ONIONS

Serves 6-8 | *Thanksgiving Feast*

For the Assembly

Place the green beans into a casserole dish and top with the cream cheese bacon sauce mixture. Place in a preheated 300-degree oven until heated through and top with fried onions.

6 cups Green bean casserole
2 cups Fried onions

For the Green Bean Casserole

1½ pounds Baby green beans, trimmed
Water as needed
Salt
1 cup Bacon, small diced
½ cup Onions, small diced
3 tablespoons Garlic, minced
½ cup All purpose flour
1 cup Heavy cream
1 cup Cream cheese, room temperature
2 cups Chicken stock
3 ounces Vegetable Oil
Salt to taste

Blanch the green beans in salted boiling water until slightly tender and shock in an ice bath. In a large sauté pan add the bacon and render until crisp. Remove the bacon fat from the pan. Add the onions and garlic to the pan and sauté for 2-3 minutes. Add the flour and cook for 2-3 minutes. Add the heavy cream and the cream cheese to a blender and puree until smooth. Add the heavy cream-cream cheese mixture to the sauté pan. Add the chicken stock and bring to a boil. Season with salt to taste and reserve hot for assembly.

For the Fried Onions

2 each Onions, thinly sliced
3 cups All purpose flour
1 teaspoon Cayenne pepper
1 teaspoon Paprika
1 teaspoon Black pepper
1 tablespoon Salt
Salt to taste

Preheat fryer oil until it reaches 375 degrees. Combine all ingredients except onions in a large mixing bowl and mix well. Separate the onions and coat thoroughly with the flour mixture. Deep fry or pan fry in preheated 375-degree oil for about 2 to 3 minutes or until golden brown and crisp. Remove from the oil and drain on paper towels, season with salt to taste.

HOMEMADE APPLE CIDER

Serves 6-8 | *Thanksgiving Feast*

For the Assembly

Pour the hot apple cider into glasses and add cinnamon sticks for garnish. Serve hot.

THE RECIPE

¾ gallon Homemade apple cider
16 each Cinnamon sticks for garnish

For the Homemade Apple Cider

6 each Green apples (Granny Smith or similar), peeled, stem and core removed, quartered
6 each Red Apples (Macintosh or similar), peeled, stem and core removed, quartered
1 cup Brandy
½ cup Sugar
3 cups Apple juice or apple cider
12 each Cloves, whole
6 each Cinnamon sticks

Place the apples and the brandy into a blender and puree until smooth. Add the apple-brandy puree, sugar, apple cider, cloves and cinnamon to a saucepot and bring to a boil. Simmer for 10-15 minutes and strain through a fine mesh sieve. Reserve hot for assembly.

PUMPKIN CRÈME BRÛLÉE AND LINZER LEAF COOKIES

Serves 6-8 | *Thanksgiving Feast*

For the Assembly

Place the crème brûlée into the center of a dessert plate and garnish with 3 linzer leaf cookies and fresh blackberries.

THE RECIPE

8 each Pumpkin crème brûlée
12 each Linzer leaf cookies
18-24 Blackberries for garnish

For the Pumpkin Crème Brûlée

4 cups Heavy cream
1 cup Sugar
2 each Vanilla beans, split
1 tablespoon Cinnamon
1 teaspoon Nutmeg
2 cups Pumpkin puree
7 each Yolks
¼ cup Sugar (to sprinkle over the top)

Preheat oven to 350 degrees. Prepare a bowl with ice and water and set aside. Bring heavy cream, sugar, vanilla beans, cinnamon, and nutmeg to a boil. In a bowl, whisk the pumpkin puree and yolks together and set aside. When the heavy cream mixture comes to boil, slowly temper the pumpkin puree-egg yolk mixture into the hot cream. Strain though a fine mesh sieve into a bowl and, using the ice bath, cool completely. Fill eight 6-ounce shallow, fluted ceramic ramekins with the créme brûlée mixture. Place ramekins into a shallow baking dish and fill with water ½ way up the sides. Bake in a preheated 350-degree oven for 20-25 minutes or until mixture is set. Place the ramekins on a tray and refrigerate until cold. Sprinkle sugar on top of the brûlée and, using a torch, melt the sugar until it caramelizes. Serve immediately.

For the Linzer Leaf Cookies

1¼ cup Unsalted butter
¾ cup Sugar
1 each Egg
1 each Yolk
½ cup Almond flour
2 cups All purpose flour
2 teaspoons Cinnamon

Preheat oven to 350 degrees. Cream the butter and the sugar together. Add the egg and the yolk slowly. Sift the almond flour and the all purpose flour together. Add the flour mixture to the butter-sugar mixture and mix until it forms a dough. Place the dough on a parchment-lined sheet pan and refrigerate. Roll out dough to about ⅛-inch thick and cut out cookies in the shape of leaves. Sprinkle with cinnamon and bake for 10-12 minutes or until edges begin to brown lightly.

The Citadel Club

In 1981, state representative Anita Hill was turned away from the club, which had restricted its facilities during lunch-time hours to men only. Due to Ms. Hill's persistence, in October 1982, full membership privileges were granted to women.

CHRISTMAS BRUNCH
The Driskill Ballroom

THE MENU

Sugar Cane and Bourbon Glazed Ham

Yukon Gold Potatoes Au Gratin and Caramelized Pearl Onions

Candied Roasted Beets and Crème Fraiche with Horseradish Mashed Parsnips

Apricot and Pear Tart

Chess Pie with Chocolate-Linzer Crust

Eggnog Tres Leches Cake

THE DRISKILL BALLROOM WAS ORIGINALLY THE GRAND SALON, the hotel's main dining room where three meals a day were served on 24 dining tables and 200 heavy walnut chairs. Beneath a 15- by 30-foot blue glass skylight, which opened to provide cooling ventilation, the Ballroom also played host to countless formal balls beginning just two weeks after the opening of the hotel with the Inaugural Ball of Governor Sul Ross.

Of the many Inaugural Balls to follow, Governor Hobby's ball in 1919 was perhaps the most spectacular, for it featured multiple orchestras playing from behind forests of ferns and lavish decorations resembling a European Court.

Today, The Driskill Ballroom remains one of the hotel's most stunning spaces. The vaulted trompe l'oeil dome required three months of work by an artist who was compared to Michelangelo as he completed the work while lying on his back. The crystal chandeliers, copied from the hotel's original gas light fixtures, have a subtle beauty. The Ballroom continues to host a range of formal and informal events including weddings, business conferences and charity functions. The Driskill's spectacular Christmas Brunch—a direct link to grand Texas celebrations of old—is also served in the Ballroom. The recipes here pay homage to Texas Christmas traditions, but with numerous small twists to update them for today's more sophisticated palates.

SUGAR CANE AND BOURBON GLAZED HAM

Serves 8 | *Christmas Brunch*

For the Assembly

Place the glazed ham onto a serving platter, garnish with fresh sage leaves and serve.

THE RECIPE

1 each Bone-in smoked ham
5 cups Sugar cane-bourbon glaze
Sage leaves for garnish

For the Ham

1 each Bone-in smoked ham
5 cups Sugar cane-bourbon glaze

Preheat oven to 350 degrees. Remove excess fat from ham and score all remaining fat. Place into a preheated 350-degree oven for 30 minutes. Thoroughly baste the ham on all sides with the sugar cane-bourbon glaze. Return to the oven and repeat this process every 30 minutes for 2–2½ hours or until the ham is cooked through.

For the Sugar Cane-Bourbon Glaze

4 cups Apple juice
1 cup Jim Beam or other bourbon
4 cups Sugar cane, peeled and crushed
2 cups Brown sugar
2 cups White sugar
1½ cups Shallots, minced
1 cup Sage, finely chopped
½ cup Cornstarch
½ cup Water
Salt to taste

Place the apple juice, bourbon, sugar cane, brown sugar, white sugar, shallots and sage into a large saucepot and bring to a boil. Mix the cornstarch and water together in a bowl and combine until it forms a cornstarch slurry. While the glaze is boiling whisk in the cornstarch slurry. Bring the glaze back to a boil and cook for 15 minutes over medium-low heat. Season with salt to taste and reserve hot to baste and glaze the ham.

YUKON GOLD POTATOES AU GRATIN AND CARAMELIZED PEARL ONIONS

Serves 8 | *Christmas Brunch*

For the Assembly

Remove the potatoes au gratin from the pan and trim edges to form a square. Place onto a serving platter, garnish with caramelized pearl onions and serve immediately.

THE RECIPE

1 recipe Yukon Gold Potatoes Au Gratin
6 cups Caramelized pearl onions

For the Yukon Gold Potatoes Au Gratin

½ cup Butter
3 tablespoons Canola oil
5 each Onions, julienned
10-15 each Yukon gold potatoes, peeled and sliced into thin discs
10 each Eggs, whipped
4 cups Heavy cream
2 tablespoons Rosemary, finely chopped
4 tablespoons Parsley, finely chopped
2 tablespoons Thyme, stems removed, finely chopped
2 cups Gruyere cheese, grated
Salt to taste

Preheat oven to 325 degrees. In a large saucepot add the butter and canola oil. Add the onions and cook over medium heat until golden brown and caramelized. Add the rosemary, parsley, and thyme to the onions and cook for 1-2 minutes. Transfer the onions and herb mixture to a large bowl and allow to cool. Add the eggs and the heavy cream to the onion mixture and combine. Add the sliced Yukon gold potatoes and half of the grated gruyere cheese to the mixture. Season with salt to taste and place into a greased, parchment paper lined square or rectangular baking dish. Tightly cover first with plastic wrap then with aluminum foil. Bake in a preheated 325-degree oven for 45 minutes to 1 hour or until the potatoes are cooked through. Remove the plastic wrap and aluminum foil and top with the remaining gruyere cheese. Place back into the oven for 5-10 minutes or until the cheese is melted and reserve hot for assembly.

For the Caramelized Pearl Onions

2 ounces Canola oil
4 ounces Whole butter, room temperature
3 cups Red pearl onions, peeled
3 cups White pearl onions, peeled
½ cup Brown sugar
½ cup Italian flat leaf parsley leaves, loosely packed
Salt to taste

In a large sauté pan add the canola oil and butter over high heat. Add the red and white pearl onions and stir. Add the brown sugar and allow to cook for 10-12 minutes over medium heat until the sugar caramelizes and the onions are tender. Place into a bowl, add the parsley leaves and toss until well combined. Season with salt to taste.

CANDIED ROASTED BEETS AND CRÈME FRAICHE
WITH HORSERADISH MASHED PARSNIPS

Serves 8 | *Christmas Brunch*

For the Assembly

Place the horseradish mashed parsnips into piping bag with a star tip and pipe in a circular fashion around a platter forming a circle. Place the candied beets into the center of the mashed parsnips and top with crème fraiche, fresh thyme and lemon zest. Garnish with fried parsnip strips and serve.

THE RECIPE

1 recipe Candied beets
1 cup Crème fraiche
Thyme sprigs for garnish
Lemon zest for garnish
6 cups Horseradish mashed parsnips
Fried parsnip strips for garnish

For the Horseradish Mashed Parsnips

3 cups Parsnips, peeled and cut into small even chunks
3 cups Idaho potatoes, peeled and cut into small even chunks
Water as needed
Salt to taste
½ cup Whole butter
½ cup Heavy cream
2-3 tablespoons Prepared horseradish
Salt to taste

Preheat oven to 350 degrees. In a saucepot add the parsnips and cover with water. Season heavily with salt and bring to a boil. Cook for 10-15 minutes or until the parsnips are cooked through. At the same time in another pot add the potatoes, cover with water and season heavily with salt. Bring to a boil and cook for 15-20 minutes or until the potatoes are cooked through. Drain both the parsnips and the potatoes and place onto a sheet pan. Place them into a preheated 350-degree oven for 5 minutes or until the parsnips and potatoes are dry. Place the butter and heavy cream into a saucepot and bring to a boil. Rice the parsnips and the potatoes into a large bowl and add the hot butter/cream mixture. Add the horseradish and stir until well combined. Season with salt to taste and reserve hot for assembly.

For the Candied Roasted Beets

1/2 cup Canola oil
Salt to taste
Pepper to taste
4 each Candy striped beets
4 each Golden beets
2 tablespoons Whole butter
1 tablespoon Canola oil
½ cup White sugar
2 tablespoons Lemon zest
2 tablespoons Thyme, stems removed, finely chopped
Salt to taste

Preheat oven to 350 degrees. Add the candy striped and golden beets to a large bowl, toss with canola oil and coat with salt and pepper to taste. Place on to a baking sheet and bake for 25-40 minutes or until fork tender. Allow the beets to cool and remove the skin. Cut the beets into equal wedges and reserve. In a large sauté pan add the whole butter and oil over high heat. Add both the cooked candy striped beets and the golden beets along with the white sugar and cook until the beets are hot and the sugar begins to caramelize. Add the lemon zest and the chopped thyme. Season with salt to taste and serve.

For the Fried Parsnip Strips

3 each Parsnips, peeled
Frying oil as needed
Salt to taste

Using a peeler, continue to peel thin strips of parsnips and place into a bowl. Heat the frying oil to 325 degrees. Add the parsnips to the preheated oil and fry until golden brown and crisp. Place the strips onto a paper towel to drain. Season with salt to taste.

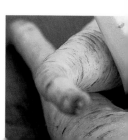

APRICOT AND PEAR TART

Serves 8-12 | *Christmas Brunch*

For the Assembly

Preheat oven to 350 degrees. Fill the tart shell half way with the Frangipan filling. Arrange the apricots, cherries, and pear in a decorative manner in the filling. Bake at 350 degrees for about 25 minutes or until golden brown. Cool completely. Lightly brush on the apricot glaze on the top of the tart and sprinkle with toasted almonds around the edge of the tart. Serve with whipped cream, cherries and pears.

THE RECIPE

1 recipe Linzer dough
1 each Frangipan tart filling
1 recipe Apricot glaze
½ cup Toasted almond slices (for garnish)
3 each Apricots, pits removed, sliced
½ cup Cherries, pits and stems removed.
1 each Pear, peeled, cored and stem removed, sliced

For the Frangipan Tart Filling

1 cup Almond paste
1½ tablespoons Sugar
½ cup Unsalted butter, softened
3 each Eggs

Using a mixer with the paddle attachment, cream the almond paste and sugar. Add butter and mix until there are no lumps present. Add the eggs slowly until incorporated. Set aside.

For the Linzer Dough

1¼ cup Unsalted butter
¾ cup Sugar
1 each Egg
1 each Yolk
½ cup Almond flour
2 cups All purpose flour

Preheat oven to 350 degrees. Cream the butter and the sugar together. Add the egg and the yolk slowly. Sift the almond flour and the all purpose flour together and add to the butter, sugar, egg mixture. Combine the ingredients until they form a dough. Place dough on a parchment-lined sheet pan and refrigerate. Roll out dough to about ⅛ inch thick and cut a circle larger than the tart pan. Place dough into pan and press into tart pan. Cut off excess dough from the edges. Freeze the shell. Cut a 12 inch circle out of parchment paper and place in the tart shell. Fill with uncooked beans. Place in the preheated oven keeping in mind that the shell should still be frozen. Bake the shell for about 10 minutes or until the shell is partially baked. Cool and set aside.

For the Apricot Glaze

1 cup Apricot preserves
¼ cup Water

Place the apricot preserves and water into a pot over medium heat until warmed through and of glaze consistency. Reserve warm for assembly.

CHESS PIE WITH CHOCOLATE-LINZER CRUST

Serves 8-12 | *Christmas Brunch*

For the Assembly

Pour the chess pie filling into the chocolate linzer crust and bake for about 45 minutes or until lightly golden brown and slightly firm to the touch. Cool completely and garnish with chantilly cream and chocolate shavings.

THE RECIPE

1 recipe Chocolate linzer crust
1 recipe Chess pie filling
2 cups Chantilly cream
1 cup Chocolate shavings

For the Chocolate Linzer Crust

½ cup Almond flour
¼ cup Chocolate cake crumbs
1 cup Cake flour
⅓ cup Cocoa powder
¼ teaspoon Baking powder
¼ teaspoon Cinnamon
1 cup Unsalted butter
¾ cup Sugar
1 each Egg
½ teaspoon Vanilla extract

Preheat the oven to 350 degrees. Sift all of the dry ingredients together and set aside. Cream the butter and the sugar until light and fluffy. Add the egg and the vanilla slowly, and mix until incorporated. Add the dry ingredients in two stages, stopping the mixer and scraping down the sides in between. Mix until combined. Chill the dough for about 2-3 hours. Roll out dough to about ⅛-inch thickness, and cut out a 12-inch circle for the 9-inch pie tin. Place dough in pie tin and fold in the edges. Using your fingers scallop or pinch the edges. Place shell into the freezer until frozen. Cut a 12-inch circle out of parchment paper and place in the pie shell. While still frozen, fill with uncooked beans and place into a 350 degree preheated oven. Bake the shell for about 10 minutes or until partially baked. Cool and set aside.

For the Chess Pie Filling

1½ cups Sugar
¼ cup Cake flour
¼ cup Unsalted butter (melted)
3 each Eggs
1 cup Buttermilk
1 teaspoon Vanilla extract

Mix together sugar and cake flour in a bowl and set aside. In a separate bowl, combine the rest of the ingredients and whisk until incorporated.

For the Chantilly Cream

2 cups Heavy whipping cream (cold)
3 tablespoons Sugar

In a mixer using the whisk attachment, add the cream and sugar and whip until stiff peaks are formed.

EGGNOG TRES LECHES CAKE

Serves 8-12 | *Christmas Brunch*

For the Assembly

Line a 10-inch cake pan with plastic wrap and place the white cake into the pan. Poke holes in the cake using a skewer and pour the eggnog mixture on the cake and wrap. Refrigerate over night. Unmold cake and place on a serving platter. Smooth on chantilly cream on all sides and cover sides with toasted pecan pieces. Dust the whole cake with powdered sugar before serving. Garnish with silver dragées if desired.

THE RECIPE

1 recipe White cake
1 recipe Tres leches eggnog
1 recipe Chantilly cream
2-3 cups Pecan pieces
½ cup Powdered sugar
½ cup Silver dragées (optional)

For the White Cake

¾ cup Shortening
1½ cups Sugar
2¼ cups Cake flour
1 tablespoon Baking powder
¾ teaspoon Salt
1 cup Milk
1½ teaspoons Vanilla extract
5 each Egg whites

Preheat oven to 350 degrees. Grease and lightly flour 10-inch cake pan. Cream the shortening and the sugar together until light and fluffy. Sift the dry ingredients together and add them alternately with the milk and vanilla. In a separate bowl, whip the egg whites to stiff peaks. Gently fold the whipped egg whites into the batter until well incorporated. Pour batter into prepared pan and smooth evenly. Bake for about 25-30 minutes or until the cake springs back. Cool completely and unmold for assembly.

For the Tres Leches Eggnog

3 each Eggs (separated)
1 tablespoon Rum
½ cup Sugar
1 cup Heavy cream
1 cup Milk
½ cup Condensed milk
¾ cup Whisky
1 each Vanilla bean (scraped, with pod)
1 teaspoon Cinnamon
2 teaspoons Nutmeg

Beat the yolks and ½ the sugar until pale yellow. In a separate bowl, combine the egg whites and the other ½ of the sugar. Whip until the egg whites reach stiff peaks. Gently fold the two egg mixtures together. Stir in the remaining ingredients until incorporated. Chill and let set overnight if possible.

For the Chantilly Cream

2 cups Heavy whipping cream (cold)
3 tablespoons Sugar

In a mixer using the whisk attachment, add the cream and sugar and whip until stiff peaks are formed.

The Driskill Ballroom

In 2001, beginning his first term, President-elect George W. Bush leased The Driskill Ballroom and Mezzanine for two weeks to hold cabinet selection meetings. His daughter, Jenna, was brought to The Driskill for safety during the 9/11 attacks.

Mrs. Price Daniel wore this satin gown for Governor
Price Daniel's second Inaugural Ball, c. 1959

NEW YEARS EVE RECEPTION
The Driskill Mezzanine

THE MENU

Fried Baby Artichokes with Ligurian Pesto

Beef Tartare and Poached Quail Egg with Hot Mustard

Caviar, Brioche, Crème Fraiche, and Micro Celery

Foie Gras-Vanilla Brûlées

Meyer Lemonade with Maple Sugar (shown right)

Strawberries and Boursin Cheese with Champagne Granita

THE SECOND FLOOR DRISKILL MEZZANINE has been the central hub of countless political and social functions, including the annual University of Texas homecoming balls. The decorations for one of the UT balls included 5,000 gardenias and maidenhair ferns. And between fifty and sixty gallons of whiskey were consumed just as a warm-up for the festivities.

Our New Year's Eve Reception updates traditional New Year's snacks with unique preparations that will generate compliments and conversation from your guests. For the best results, you need to choose the finest ingredients—don't cut corners on high-quality caviar and champagne. Finally, use your imagination to choose the best serving utensils to match with each dish. The result will be an elegant evening guaranteed to ring in a happy new year.

FRIED BABY ARTICHOKES WITH LIGURIAN PESTO

Serves 12 | *New Years Eve Reception*

For the Assembly

On 12 large dessert or soup spoons, place a small dollop of the pesto in the base of each spoon. Place the fried artichokes on top of the pesto, garnish with one toasted pinenut, and sprinkle with grated Parmesan cheese.

THE RECIPE

12 each Fried baby artichokes
½ cup Ligurian pesto
2 tablespoons Parmesan cheese, grated
12 each Pinenuts, lightly toasted

For the Fried Baby Artichokes

12 each Blanched artichokes
¼ cup Milk
1 cup Eggs, whipped
½ cup Semolina flour
¼ cup Bread crumbs
½ cup All purpose flour
Salt to taste

Preheat fryer oil to 350 degrees. Mix the milk with the whipped eggs and combine. Mix the semolina flour and the bread crumbs together. Using a standard breading procedure, dredge the artichokes into the flour, dip into the egg wash and dredge into the semolina-bread crumb mixture. Place into preheated 350-degree frying oil and fry until golden brown and crisp. Remove the artichokes from the oil and place onto paper towels. Season with salt to taste and serve immediately.

For the Blanched Artichokes

Water as needed
2 each Lemons, sliced
Salt to taste
4 each Baby artichokes, outer leaves removed, quartered

Bring the water, lemons and salt to a boil. Add the quartered artichokes and cook for 3-5 minutes or until fork tender. Shock in an ice bath and drain.

For the Ligurian Pesto

3 each Garlic cloves, peeled
1 tablespoon Pine nuts, lightly toasted
½ cup Extra virgin olive oil
¼ cup Parmesan cheese, grated
3 each Lemons, juiced and zested
1 cup Basil leaves, tightly packed, stems removed
1 cup Mint leaves, tightly packed, stems removed
Salt to taste

Place the garlic, pine nuts, olive oil, parmesan, lemon juice and lemon zest into a food processor or blender and puree until very smooth. While the machine is running, add the basil leaves and mint leaves. Puree for as short a time as possible and until the desired consistency is reached. Season with salt to taste.

BEEF TARTARE AND POACHED QUAIL EGG WITH HOT MUSTARD

Serves 12 | *New Years Eve Reception*

For the Assembly

Place the beef tartare into small serving spoons. Place the poached quail egg on top of the tartare. Top with a small dollop of hot mustard and sprigs of burgundy amaranth.

THE RECIPE

1½ cups Beef tartare
12 each Poached quail eggs
1 tablespoon Hot mustard
Burgundy amaranth for garnish (optional)

For the Beef Tartare

1½ cups Beef tenderloin, small diced, chilled
1 teaspoon Shallots, finely minced
1 teaspoon Ginger, peeled and finely minced
1 teaspoon Green onions, finely chopped
½ teaspoon Sesame oil
1 teaspoon Hot mustard
Salt to taste

Place all ingredients into a bowl and mix well. Season with salt to taste and serve immediately.

For the Poached Quail Eggs

12 each Quail eggs
Water as needed
¼ cup White wine vinegar

Bring water and white wine vinegar to a boil in a large saucepot and then turn down to a simmer over medium heat. Slowly and carefully crack the quail eggs 2-3 at a time into the water and cook for 1-2 minutes or until the eggs reach soft boiled. Remove the eggs and shock them in an ice bath. Remove from the ice bath and drain on a paper towel, reserve cold for assembly.

CAVIAR, BRIOCHE, CRÈME FRAICHE, AND MICRO CELERY

Serves 12 | *New Years Eve Reception*

For the Assembly

Spread the crème fraiche evenly over the brioche croutons. Place a dollop of caviar on top of the crème fraiche and top with micro celery.

THE RECIPE

1 ounce Caviar, ossetra or similar
12 each Brioche croutons
¼ cup Crème fraiche
¼ cup Micro celery (may substitute celery leaves)

For the Brioche Croutons

2 cups Eggs
1 cup Milk
1 cup All purpose flour
3½ cups Bread flour
1½ tablespoon Instant yeast
3 tablespoon Sugar
2½ teaspoon Salt
3 each Eggs
6 tablespoons water
2¼ cups Butter, cubed and softened

Preheat oven to 375 degrees. Place all the ingredients, except the butter, in a mixer with the dough hook attachment. Turn mixer on speed 1 for 2 minutes, then speed 2 for 6 minutes. While on speed 2, add the butter in small pieces. Mix until incorporated and the dough forms a ball. Take dough out of mixer and let rest on table. Cover with plastic wrap and allow to rest for 5-10 minutes. Pan spray loaf pans. Shape dough and place in pans. Cover and proof in a warm place until the loaves double in size. Mix the eggs and water together to form an egg wash and brush the top of the brioche. Bake in a preheated 375-degree oven for 25-30 minutes or until golden brown. Remove from oven and allow to completely cool. Cut into small circles using a fluted cutter and brush with butter. Place onto a baking sheet and toast in a preheated 375-degree oven until slightly crisp.

FOIE GRAS-VANILLA BRÛLÉES

Serves 12-24 | *New Years Eve Reception*

For the Assembly

Sprinkle a teaspoon of sugar on top
of the foie gras vanilla mix and, using a
blowtorch, caramelize the very top layer.
Serve immediately.

THE RECIPE

24 each Foie gras-vanilla brûlées
White sugar as needed

For the Foie Gras-Vanilla Brûlées

¼ lb. Foie gras, veins removed, diced
2 cups Heavy cream
1 each Vanilla bean, split
1 teaspoon Vanilla extract
5 each Egg yolks

Preheat oven to 325 degrees. Heat a large saute pan over high
heat and saute the diced foie gras for one minute or until golden
brown. Allow to cool slightly and place the sauteed foie gras and
all foie gras fat into a blender. Scrape the seeds from the vanilla
bean and combine with the heavy cream and the vanilla extract.
Add the cream-vanilla mixture to the foie gras and puree until
smooth. Add the egg yolks, puree until smooth and season with
salt to taste. Spoon the mixture into the egg cups or other small
ovenproof dish and place into a shallow baking dish. Fill the
baking dish half way with water and cover tightly with aluminum
foil. Place into a preheated 325-degree oven for 60-70 minutes
or until the mixture is firm to the touch. Allow to cool completely
and reserve for assembly.

MEYER LEMONADE WITH MAPLE SUGAR

Serves 12 | *New Years Eve Reception*

For the Assembly

Place tall shot glasses into the freezer until completely chilled. Dip the top edges into the maple sugar to coat the rim of each glass. Carefully pour the cold meyer lemonade into the glasses and serve immediately.

THE RECIPE

12 each Meyer lemonade shooters
2 tablespoons Maple sugar

For the Meyer Lemonade

3 cups Meyer lemon juice
½ cup Sugar

Mix the meyer lemon juice and sugar together. Place into the freezer until completely chilled but not frozen. Serve ice cold.

STRAWBERRIES AND BOURSIN CHEESE WITH CHAMPAGNE GRANITA

Serves 12 | *New Years Eve Reception*

For the Assembly

Cut off the tops of the strawberries and reserve. Scoop out the center of the strawberry bottom using a melon baller. Fill and stuff the strawberry bottoms with the boursin cheese and refrigerate until completely cold. Top the boursin cheese with the champagne granita and place the strawberry tops back on top of the strawberry bottoms. Serve immediately.

THE RECIPE

12 each Long-stem strawberries
1/2 cup Boursin cheese, room temperature
1/2 cup Champagne granita

For the Champagne Granita

1/2 cup Water
1/2 cup Sugar
1 cup Champagne

Mix the water and sugar together in a small saucepot. Bring mixture to a boil and allow to completely cool. Add the champagne and place into a shallow pan. Place into a freezer until completely frozen. Using a spoon or fork scrape the granita into ice shavings.

The Driskill Mezzanine

Mezzanine restoration started in 1996. The columns were painted and then "marbleized" using turkey feathers as paint brushes in the style of the 1880s. Turkey feathers and badger hair brushes were chosen for their extreme softness.

DRISKILL HOTEL
Host to famous Texans since 1886. Scene of Inaugural Ball for Gov. L. S. "Sul" Ross, Jan. 1887; Inaugural Balls for later Governors, as well as many other state and civic social affairs. Entertains Presidents, other national figures, foreign diplomats, artists, leaders in business and professions.

(1966)

epilogue

clockwise from upper left - The Texas Capitol, c. 1881-1888; fire destroys the top of the annex (it was never rebuilt), c. 1952; Driskill manager, Charles P. Shadbolt, c. 1897; detail from Driskill stock certificate, c. 1972; brochure pictures , c. 1970's.

EXCERPT FROM "A COWBOY'S PRAYER"

Oh, Lord, I know that others find you in the light
And yet I seem to find you near tonight
In this dim quiet starlight on the plains

Let me be easy on the man that's down
Let me be fair and generous with all
But never let them say I'm mean or small

Make me as big and open as the plains
As honest as the horse between my knees
Clean as the wind that blows behind the rains
Free as the hawk that circles the breeze

Just keep an eye on all that's done or said
And right me sometimes when I turn aside
And guide me on the long dim trail ahead
That stretches upward, toward the Great Divide.

–BADGER CLARK, (PUBLISHED 1906)

When it's time for you to leave us,
May your memories be pleasant
And your journey safe –

Happy Trails,
The Management & Staff
The Driskill Hotel

left, top to bottom - detail from Christmas dinner menu, c. 1897;
detail from Father's Day menu, c. 1961.

right, top to bottom - Victorian Suite, today; Capitol Suite, today;
Renaissance Bridal Suite, today.

index

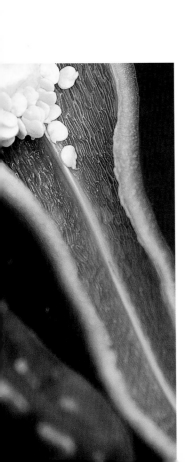

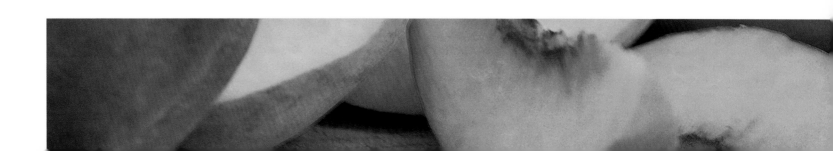

index

acknowledgements

Publishing *The Driskill Hotel: Stories of Austin's Legendary Hotel/A Cookbook for Special Occasions*
required the help of many dedicated people. The Driskill would like to thank the following:

- Matt Hovis, Marissa Quintans, KevinWhitley & David Schlickeisen,
  Action Figure. This book embodies the sophisticated aesthetic of your
  gifted designers, thank you for your commitment.

- Mark Knight & Taggart Sorenson, Mark Knight Photography.
  Your imagery and artistic vision have been instrumental in capturing
  the beautiful spirit of The Driskill.

- Our entire Driskill team, especially, John Langston, Richard Osaze-Ediae,
  Elizabeth Krauss, Jeffrey Rhein, Joyce Benavidez and the culinary staff for
  their vision, creativity and wisdom.

- All of the dedicated Recipe Testers:
  Thank you for your long hours and hard work. Your educated palates
  provided valuable input into the final drafting of each recipe.

We would also like to thank the following for their dedication during the
most recent restoration of The Driskill Hotel:

Bill Fowler & Mark Rawlings, HHCC, Inc., General Contractors
Marla Bommarito & Judith Bush, The Bommarito Group, Inc.
Candace Volz, Volz & Associates, Inc.
Bryant Stanton, Stanton Glass Studio, LLC
Joanne Counihan and Michael T. Counihan, Counihan & Associates
Larry Kleinkemper, Architectural Vision
Joe Barbieri, Artist
Victor L. Fuller, Charles W. Broeman, II, Stephen M. Fuller,
Ed Morin and Stephen Wright, Brothers Property Corporation